Traverse Theatre Company

Pandas

By Rona Munro

Cast

Andy	Keith Fleming
Madeleine	Meg Fraser
Jie Hui	Siu Hun Li
Julie	Vicki Liddelle
James	Phil McKee
Lin Han	Crystal Yu

Director	Rebecca Gatward
Assistant Director	David Betz-Heinemann
Designer	Liz Cooke
Lighting Designer	Colin Grenfell
Sound Designer	John Harris
Dramaturg	Katherine Mendelsohn

Stage Manager	Daniel Dixon
Deputy Stage Manager	Ria Tubman
Assistant Stage Manager	Naomi Stalker
Wardrobe Supervisor	Sarah Holland
Wardrobe Assistant	Helen Gallogly

**First performed at the Traverse Theatre
Friday 15 April 2011**

A Traverse Theatre Commission

THE TRAVERSE

Artistic Director: Dominic Hill

The Traverse has an unrivalled reputation for producing contemporary theatre of the highest quality, invention and energy, and for its dedication to new writing.
(Scotland on Sunday)

The Traverse is Scotland's New Writing Theatre. From its conception in 1963, it has embraced a spirit of innovation and risk-taking that launched the careers of many of Scotland's best-known writers including John Byrne, David Greig, David Harrower and Liz Lochhead. It is unique in Scotland in that it fulfils the crucial role of providing the infrastructure, professional support and expertise to ensure the development of a dynamic theatre culture for Scotland. It commissions and develops new plays or adaptations from contemporary playwrights. It produces, on average, six Traverse Theatre Company productions or co-productions per year. It also presents a large number of productions from visiting companies from across the UK. These include new plays, adaptations, dance, physical theatre, puppetry and contemporary music.

The Traverse is a pivotal venue in Edinburgh and this is particularly the case during the Edinburgh Festival in August – positioned as it is between the Edinburgh Festival Fringe and the Edinburgh International Festival.

The Traverse is also the home of the Manipulate Visual Theatre Festival, the Bank of Scotland Imaginate Festival and the Traverse's own autumn Festival.

A Rolls-Royce machine for promoting new Scottish drama across Europe and beyond. (The Scotsman)

The Traverse's work with young people is of major importance and takes the form of encouraging playwriting through its flagship education project, Class Act, as well as the Young Writers' Group. Class Act recently celebrated its twenty-first anniversary and has given school pupils the opportunity to develop their plays with professional playwrights and work with directors and actors to see the finished pieces performed on stage at the Traverse. The hugely successful Young Writers' Group is open to new writers aged 18–25. Scribble offers an after-school playwriting and theatre-skills workshop for 14–17 year olds. Both programmes are led by professional playwrights.

Traverse Theatre (Scotland) Limited, registered in Scotland SC 076037.
Registered Charity No. SC 002368, VAT reg. no. 356 0682 47.
Registered Office: Traverse Theatre, Cambridge Street, Edinburgh, EH1 2ED.

COMPANY BIOGRAPHIES

David Betz-Heinemann (Assistant Director)
David is resident Assistant Director at the Traverse Theatre and Artistic Director of People at Play. Directing credits include: *Four Parts Broken* (Òran Mór/National Theatre of Scotland); *Tales from the Kalevala* (with London Arts Orchestra); *Every Girl, Life Without Music, Duty, The End of the Beginning* (National Theatre Studio); *Widescream, Looking In, Vita the Vamp* (Old Vic New Voices); *Disco Pigs, Talking to Terrorists* (Stephen Joseph, Scarborough, NSDF); *The Cradle, Kiss Me Kate* (New Theatre, Nottingham) and *Dancing at Lughnasa* (Edinburgh Festival/Epsom Playhouse Festival). Assisting credits for the Traverse Theatre include: *Class Act 21*, Dominic Hill on *The Three Musketeers and the Princess of Spain*, Vicky Featherstone and Stewart Laing on *Impossible Things Before Breakfast*. Other assisting work includes: Mike Bradwell on *The Big Script* (Soho Theatre, London); Andrew Breakwell on *Tom's Midnight Garden* (Nottingham Playhouse) and Christopher Ettridge on *Figaro Gets Divorced* (Cochrane Theatre, London).

Liz Cooke (Designer)
Liz trained at Slade School of Fine Art and Oxford University. Work for the Traverse: *Greenfield*. Other design work includes: *Othello, The Indian Boy, Thyestes* (Royal Shakespeare Company); *Bleak House, Humble Boy, The Wicked Lady, The Weir* (New Vic, Staffordshire); *The Merchant of Venice, Pericles, The Comedy of Errors, Much Ado About Nothing* (Shakespeare's Globe); *Monkey!, The Accrington Pals, And All the Children Cried* (West Yorkshire Playhouse); *Pirates!* (Polka Theatre, London); *Stop Messing About* (West End/tour); *Touched, The Invention of Love, The Beauty Queen of Leenane* (Salisbury Playhouse); *Virgins, Theatre Cafe* (Company of Angels); *Little Wolf's Book of Badness, The Schuman Plan* (Hampstead Theatre, London); *Ma Vie En Rose* (Young Vic, London); *Performances* (Wilton's Music Hall); *Shadowmouth* (Sheffield Crucible); *Yikes!* (Unicorn Theatre, London); *Saucy Jack and the Space Vixens* (West End); *NHS the Musical* (Drum Theatre, Plymouth); *The Little Mermaid* (Sphinx); *Badnuff* (Soho Theatre, London); *Peter Pan* (Oxford Playhouse); *A Whistle in the Dark* (Citizens' Theatre, Glasgow); *Eldorado* (National Theatre of Prague); *Damages* (Bush Theatre, London); *The Gift* (Birmingham Rep/Tricycle Theatre, London); *Round the Horne – Revisited* (West End/tour); *The Birds* (National Theatre, London); *The Magic Toyshop* (Shared Experience); *The Hackney Office* (Druid); *Les Blancs* (Royal Exchange, Manchester); *Spoonface Steinberg* (West End); *The Glory of Living* (Royal Court Theatre, London); *Volunteers* (Gate Theatre, London).

Keith Fleming (*Andy*)

Keith's work for the Traverse: *The Dark Things*. Other theatre work includes: *Black Watch, Peer Gynt* (co-produced with Dundee Rep); *Miracle Man* (National Theatre of Scotland); *Doubt, Autobahn* (Theatre Jezebel); *Barflies* (Grid Iron); *Trumpets and Raspberries* (Royal Lyceum, Edinburgh); *Sunshine on Leith, Scenes from an Execution, Cabaret, Mince, Twelfth Night, Macbeth, Rum and Vodka* (Dundee Rep). In 2008 Keith was nominated for Best Actor at the TMA Awards and won Best Actor – Critics' Award for Theatre in Scotland.

Meg Fraser (*Madeleine*)

Meg trained at RSAMD. Work for the Traverse includes: *Nova Scotia, Fall, Cockroach* (co-produced with the National Theatre of Scotland); *Hans & Freda* (co-produced by Puppet Lab); *T5, All is Vanity* (co-produced with Hibrow Productions). Other theatre work includes: *Four Parts Broken* (Òran Mór/National Theatre of Scotland); *The Silver Darlings* (His Majesty's Theatre, Aberdeen and Scottish tour); *The Lion, the Witch and the Wardrobe, All My Sons* (TMA Best Supporting Performer, 2007), *The Taming of the Shrew, Julius Caesar, Playboy of the Western World* (Royal Lyceum, Edinburgh); *Tom Fool* (Citizens' Theatre; Critics' Award for Theatre, Best Female Performance, 2007); *Hamlet, Macbeth, As You Like It, Twelfth Night, Young People's Macbeth, Eric La Rue* (Royal Shakespeare Company); *Being Norwegian* (Òran Mór/Paines Plough); *The Winter's Tale, A Midsummer Night's Dream, The Night Before Christmas, Mince, The Seagull* and *Cabaret* (Dundee Rep). Meg was also part of the original three-year ensemble at Dundee Rep. Television and film work includes: *Young Adam, Ever Here I Be* (Digicult); *Taggart: Island; Wanting and Getting* (GFVW); *Life Support, Comedy Nation* (BBC); *Taggart: Atonement* (STV). Radio includes: *Tough Love, Gonwanaland, Seeing is Believing, The Meek, An Expert in Murder, The Tenderness of Wolves, The Trick is to Keep Breathing* (BBC).

Rebecca Gatward (Director)

Rebecca is a freelance television and theatre director. Theatre work includes: *The Comedy of Errors, The Merchant of Venice* (Shakespeare's Globe); *The Indian Boy* (also by Rona Munro), *The Canterbury Tales, Thyestes* (Royal Shakespeare Company); *Touched* (Salisbury Playhouse); *Yikes!* (Unicorn Theatre, London); *Cancer Tales* (New Wolsey Theatre Studio); *Old King Cole* (Unicorn at the Cochrane Theatre, London); *The Accrington Pals* (West Yorkshire Playhouse); *The Owl Who Was Afraid of the Dark* (Bristol Old Vic); *The Magic Toyshop* (Shared Experience); *The Three Birds* (Gate Theatre, London/Royal National Theatre Studio; Winner of Time Out Live Award for Most Outstanding Talent Off-West End, 2000); *Venecia* (Gate Theatre, London). In 2002 she directed Matt Damon and Casey Affleck in *This is Our Youth* (Garrick Theatre, London). Television work includes: *Doctors, EastEnders, Casualty* (BBC).

Colin Grenfell (Lighting Designer)

Colin's work for the Traverse: *Unprotected*. Other theatre work includes: *Playing the Victim* (Told by an Idiot); *Black Watch, The Bacchae* (co-produced with Edinburgh International Festival), *365* (National Theatre of Scotland); *Macbeth, Canary* (co-produced with Hampstead Theatre, London; Liverpool Everyman); *Le Nozze di Figaro, La Rondine, Fidelio, Don Giovanni, Carmen, Pelléas et Mélisande, La Bohème, Un Ballo in Maschera* (Opera Holland Park); *A Doll's House, Equus* (Dundee Rep); *The Beauty Queen of Leenane* (Royal Lyceum, Edinburgh); *I am Yusuf and This is My Brother, No Idea* (co-produced with Improbable Theatre; Young Vic, London); *Faith, Cold Reading* (Live Theatre, Newcastle); *Through a Glass Darkly, When the Rain Stops Falling* (Almeida Theatre, London); *The Glass Menagerie* (Salisbury Playhouse/Shared Experience); *The Caretaker* (Trafalgar Studios, London); *Baby Baby* (Stellar Quines); *Mine* (Hampstead Theatre, London); *Silver Birch House* (Arcola Theatre); *Separate Tables, Kes* (Royal Exchange, Manchester); *Theatre of Blood* (National Theatre, London); *Body Talk* (Royal Court, London).

John Harris (Sound Designer)

John's work for the Traverse: *While You Lie, Any Given Day, The Dark Things, The Nest, Knives in Hens, Anna Weiss, East Coast Chicken Supper, Family, Perfect Days, Greta, Sharp Shorts, Kill The Old, Torture their Young, The Last Witch* (co-produced with Edinburgh International Festival), *The Garden* and *Lucky Box* (co-produced with Òran Mór), *Nobody Will Ever Forgive Us, Nasty Brutish and Short* and *The Dogstone* (co-produced with National Theatre of Scotland). Other theatre work includes: *Monaciello* (Tron Theatre, Glasgow/Naples International Theatre Festival); *Julie, Mary Stuart* (National Theatre of Scotland); *The Firebird, Mother Courage, Jack and the Beanstalk* (Dundee Rep); *Jerusalem* (West Yorkshire Playhouse); *Midwinter, Solstice* (Royal Shakespeare Company). Opera includes: *Death of a Scientist* (Scottish Opera 5:15 series); *Sleep Sleep/What is She?/The Sermon* (Tapestry Opera Theatre). Film and television work includes: *The Fingertrap* (BAFTA Scotland Emerging Talent Award, 2009); *Saltmark* (Blindside); *The Emperor, The Green Man of Knowledge* (Red Kite). Other commissions include: music for the Scottish Flute Trio, Red Note Ensemble and Hebrides Ensemble. John was for several years assistant organist at St Giles' Cathedral, Edinburgh, and took his Masters degree in composition at the RSAMD in Glasgow.

Siu Hun Li (*Jie Hui*)

Siu Hun trained at RADA. Theatre work includes: *365* (National Theatre of Scotland); *Coalition* (Theatre503). Television work includes: *Casualty, Spirit Warriors* (BBC). Film work includes: *Johnny English Reborn* (Working Title); *Foster* (Kintop Pictures); *Perfect Sense* (Sigma Films); *My Dad the Communist* (B3 Media/Short Film).

Vicki Liddelle (*Julie*)

Vicki's work for the Traverse: *The Last Witch, San Diego* (both co-produced with Edinburgh International Festival), *Kyoto* (co-produced with Òran Mór), *King of the Fields*. Other theatre work includes: *Casanova* (Suspect Culture); *Passing Places* (Derby Playhouse); *Britannia Rules* (Royal Lyceum, Edinburgh); *The Glass Menagerie* (Dundee Rep); *The Suicide* (Communicado). Vicki recently finished filming *Case Histories* for the BBC. Television and film work includes: *Garrow's Law, Dear Green Place, Suspect, Jess the Border Collie, The Big Tease*. Vicki has worked extensively in radio drama and co-wrote the comedy pilot *Blow Me Beautiful* for BBC Radio Scotland.

Phil McKee (*James*)

Phil's work for the Traverse includes: *Any Given Day, Strawberries in January* (co-produced with Paines Plough). Other theatre work includes: *That Face* (Tron Theatre, Glasgow); *Relocated* (Royal Court, London); *Noughts & Crosses* (Royal Shakespeare Company); *Mary Stuart* (National Theatre of Scotland); *A Mad Man Sings to the Moon, Julius Caesar* (Royal Lyceum, Edinburgh); *Damages, Stitching* (Bush Theatre, London); *8000m* (Suspect Culture); *Macbeth* (Landor Theatre); *The Boat Plays, The Robbers* (Gate Theatre, London); *Richard III, King Lear, Napoli Milonaria* (National Theatre, London); *Lady Betty* (Cheek by Jowl). Television work includes *Garrow's Law, Silent Witness, Lost in France, Crime Traveller, Lovejoy* (BBC); *Taggart, Family, Heartbeat, Soldier, Soldier, The Bill* (ITV); *Ghost Squad* (Channel 4); *Band of Brothers* (HBO); *The Place of the Dead* (LWT); *Richard II* (Illuminations). Film work includes: *Clash of the Titans* (Warner Bros); *The Shepherd* (Sony Pictures); *Joan of Arc* (Gaumont Pictures); *The Lost Battalion* (A&E); *The Debt Collector* (Channel 4 Films); *George & the Dragon* (Apollo Media); *The Star* (Renegade Films). Phil has also worked on radio plays for BBC Radio 3 and 4.

Rona Munro (Writer)

Rona has written extensively for stage, radio, film and television. Work for the Traverse includes: *The Last Witch* (co-produced with Edinburgh International Festival), *Fugue, Iron* and a translation of Évelyne de Chenelière's *Strawberries in January*. Other plays include: *Bold Girls* (7:84); *The Maiden Stone* (Hampstead Theatre, London); *Long Time Dead* (Paines Plough); adaptations of *Mary Barton* and *Watership Down* (Royal Exchange, Manchester/Lyric Hammersmith); a contemporary version of *The House of Bernarda Alba* (National Theatre of Scotland). Television and film work includes: *Ladybird Ladybird* (directed by Ken Loach); *Aimee and Jaguar* and television dramas *Rehab* and the BAFTA nominated *Bumping the Odds* for the BBC. Rona has also written many single plays for radio and television and contributed to series such as *Casualty* and *Doctor Who*.

She is co-founder and resident writer for Scotland's longest-running small-scale touring theatre company, *The MsFits,* whose most recent production *Mad Bad and Dangerous to Know* began a tour throughout the UK in March 2011. Her play *Little Eagles* (Royal Shakespeare Company) opened at Hampstead Theatre in April 2011. She also wrote the screenplay for the film *Oranges and Sunshine*, directed by Jim Loach and starring Emily Watson which went on general release in April 2011. Rona previously worked with *Pandas* director Rebecca Gatward on *The Indian Boy* in 2006.

Crystal Yu (*Lin Han*)

Born in Hong Kong, Crystal first came to the UK at the age of eleven after being awarded a place at Elmhurst School of Dance and Performing Arts. This is Crystal's first time working with the Traverse Theatre Company. Other theatre work includes: *Spring Celebration* (ChinaWest International Productions); *Miss Saigon* (UK and European tour); *Burning Maps* (Outside Edge Theatre); *The Youth of Old Age* (The Wireless Theatre Company); *Bouncers* (Freeflow Productions); *After Juliet* (Geoffrey Swann/Camberley Theatre). Television and film work includes: *Will*; *Shanghai* (with John Cusack and Chow Yun-Fat); *Casualty, Spirit Warriors* (BBC); *Museum Future 2058, Diamond Geezer* (ITV). Crystal has also appeared in a variety of international commercials for brands including HSBC, Danone Aqua, MTV, Nokia, Orange, and most notably appearing alongside Madonna in a campaign for her H&M fashion line.

SUPPORT THE TRAVERSE

We would like to thank the following
corporate sponsors for their recent support

New Arts Sponsorship Grants
Supported by the Scottish Government
In conjunction with

A&B
Arts & Business Scotland

For their generous support, the Traverse thanks our Devotees
Joan Aitken, Stewart Binnie, Katie Bradford, Fiona Bradley,
Adrienne Sinclair Chalmers, Lawrence Clark, Adam Fowler, Joscelyn Fox,
Caroline Gardner, John Knight OBE, Iain Millar, Gillian Moulton, Helen Pitkethly,
Michael Ridings, Bridget Stevens

Emerging Playwright on Attachment post supported by Playwrights' Studio, Scotland
as a Partnership Project

Pearson Playwright supported by **Pearson**

For their continued generous support of Traverse productions, the Traverse thanks
Camerabase, Paterson SA Hairdressing, Stems Florist

To find out how you can support the Traverse, please contact Fiona Sturgeon Shea,
Head of Communications, on 0131 228 3223 or
fiona.sturgeonshea@traverse.co.uk

The Traverse Theatre's work
would not be possible without the support of

For their help on *Pandas*, the company would like to thank
David Sneddon at the Tron, Jess Richards at the National Theatre of Scotland,
Street Lighting Edinburgh City Council, O2 at St James Shopping Centre, Macrobert

TRAVERSE THEATRE – THE COMPANY

PANDAS

Rona Munro

For Dave

Author's Note

Once in a while you write a play and you can't pinpoint where it comes from. With *Pandas* the characters simply demanded to start talking about love. That was the start, but this play came bouncing joyfully out of other places as well. It comes from a long and happy relationship with the Traverse Theatre, I couldn't imagine this play starting its life anywhere else. It comes out of an abiding love affair with the city of Edinburgh. I might have been born in Aberdeen but when the cherry blossom comes out on The Meadows there's nowhere else on Earth I'd rather be. But, more than anywhere else, this play comes out of the twenty-five years I've spent writing comedies for MsFits theatre company and the wonderful Fiona Knowles. Without Fiona and without those years writing for an actress with such superb storytelling skills, my own would never have been able to develop so happily. Bless you, darling, this one's for you too.

In the delightful event that you have this script in your hands with a view to further production a few explanations and safety warnings. The scene descriptions may induce headaches in any designer (not to mention sound and lighting designers). What's important is that the audience gets an impression of springtime, green trees and blossom. How that's achieved is not crucial nor are any mentioned effects or sound effects.

Also, as a note to actors and directors, what we discovered in rehearsal was that it's crucial to pin down who knows what and when they know it... and to mark the moment each character *really* falls in love.

Rona Munro

Characters

JAMES
JULIE
JIE HUI
LIN HAN
ANDY
MADELEINE

Note on Text

Speeches in Mandarin are written phonetically. Jie Hui and Lin Han speak actual Mandarin where specified, the rest of the time Lin Han is usually speaking Mandarin (as English for audience comprehension) unless it specifies English. Jie Hui speaks English to all the other characters and Mandarin to Lin Han unless otherwise indicated.

The change from one language to the other occurs wherever it feels fluid and allows comprehension for the audience, but we found it useful to switch from one language to another in the middle of a speech rather than the end. This seems to make the device clearer for an audience.

This text went to press before the end of rehearsals and so may differ slightly from the play as performed.

ACT ONE

There's a tree. It could be strands of thin bamboo towering to forest height, it could be an old urban trunk leaning over the roofs, it could be a cherry tree laden with blossom. It will be all of these things. Its leaves and branches are dancing, moving, flickering. Wind in leaves dying away to a faint, bleating call… the sound of the giant panda.

Fade lights into: An immaculate living room.

JAMES, *a forty-something detective is caught in the process of creeping into his own house, lights on, caught in the glare like a guilty burglar.* JULIE, *late thirties, his partner, is standing by the light switch. There are neat heaps of boxes everywhere.*

JULIE. What's that?

JAMES. What's what?

JULIE. On your jacket? What's that on your jacket?

   JAMES *looks for a moment.*

JAMES. I think it's somebody's brains.

JULIE. What have I told you about coming home with somebody's brains on your jacket?

JAMES. Sorry.

JULIE. Have I not told you?

JAMES. You have. Sorry.

JULIE. So you don't remember or you don't care?

   Pause.

JAMES. I couldn't help it.

JULIE. What do you think that's like for me?

JAMES. Sorry.

JULIE. This is the whole thing, the whole thing right here, James, right here, this is why I have to go. What do you think it's like for me, you tracking someone else's brains into the house?

JAMES. It's only a wee bit…

JULIE. It's disgusting!

JAMES. It was a mistake. I had to secure the scene…

JULIE. Heard it! *Heard it!*

JAMES. You couldny avoid it was… it was… all over…

JULIE. How fucking pissed are you?

Pause.

JAMES. On a scale of one to ten?

Waits, no response.

About an eight.

Still nothing.

Eight point five… mebbe.

JULIE. You went to the pub with some poor soul's brains on your jacket?

JAMES. That's *why* I went to the pub! That's *why!*

JULIE. Heard it! *Heard it!*

JAMES. What do you mean you have to go?

Beat.

JULIE (*change of tone*). Och James…

JAMES. What do you mean?

JULIE. Come on.

JAMES. You're leaving me? You're *leaving* me?

JULIE. What did you think we'd been talking about?

JAMES. Sorting things out.

JULIE. Well… maybe I've done a bit more sorting out than you.

JAMES. Wait… just…

JULIE. James…

JAMES. *Wait!*

> *He's pulling off his jacket. Exits.*

> *Clattering, banging and swearing offstage, then* JAMES *re-enters, without his jacket.*

(*Breathless.*) There! It's in the bin.

JULIE. James…

JAMES. The jacket is in the bin. Crucial fucking DNA evidence and all.

JULIE. It's not crucial evidence, is it? You wouldn't have binned it if it was crucial. It wouldn't have been on your jacket if it was crucial, it's just another bit of the… vile… filthy… *horror* that you track into the house along with the whisky fumes!

JAMES. Don't leave me, Julie.

JULIE. I've got to.

JAMES. Don't leave me.

JULIE. I've got to.

JAMES. Please.

JULIE. I've got to.

JAMES. Please. Please.

JULIE. I've got to.

> *Beat.*

JAMES. No you don't.

JULIE. I do.

JAMES. You don't.

JULIE. I *do*!

JAMES. But why? Why?

JULIE. I can't talk about this any more, I can't… No more! No. More.

JAMES. But I love you.

JULIE. I know you do, James. I know.

JAMES. And you love me.

JULIE. Not the same way.

JAMES. What does that matter?

What do you mean?

Aye, you do! You do!

JULIE. Come on now, stop this. Come to bed.

JAMES. So… you're not leaving?

JULIE. In the morning.

JAMES. In the morning!? In the morning!? If you're fucking leaving go now, know what I mean? If you canny stand this life, this love, this man, then run, run away! Don't be… *friendly* about it! Don't rip my heart out and then offer me a cup of tea! Go! Don't just be hanging round for a cheaper taxi fare.

JULIE. I'm taking the car.

JAMES. Oh… right.

JULIE. Well… I mean you're getting possession of the flat.

JAMES. Uh-huh.

JULIE. And we can talk about how we sort it all out as and when.

JAMES. As and when what?

JULIE. As and when we see where we are.

Beat.

JAMES. I'm right here! I'm right here, Julie, and I love you!

Beat.

JULIE. I have to go.

JAMES. *You don't!*

JULIE. I can't do this. I need to sleep.

JAMES. At least give me a reason I can understand.

JULIE. If you could understand I wouldn't have to leave.

JAMES. *Anything!*

JULIE. You have someone's brains on your jacket and you
smell like an ashtray full of whisky.

JAMES. The jacket's away!

JULIE. And for you that's change. I'm looking for something
more fundamental.

JAMES. You knew what I was like the first night. You said
you'd love me for ever. You said you never wanted me to
change!

JULIE. I meant it when I said it.

JAMES. But now you don't?

JULIE. No.

JAMES. Then you're the one that's changed. Aren't you?

JULIE. I just want one thing, one thing I can hold onto that's…
beautiful.

JAMES. Beautiful.

JULIE. Yes.

JAMES. Did you not like those earrings then…

JULIE (*cutting him off*). James, all I can rely on you to bring home is depression and a hangover. And it's not as if you're ever going to get anything out of it except a pension, is it? It's not like you're going to run off to China to make a million.

JAMES. Eh?

JULIE. You know what I mean.

JAMES. I have no fucking idea what you mean.

JULIE. Alright, just… you know… something like that.

JAMES. Like what?

JULIE. Anything!

JAMES. Like getting on a plane to China and making a million pounds?

JULIE. Or anything!

JAMES. No, that was a bit fucking specific actually. You're going to China?

JULIE. Of course not.

Beat.

Why would I go to China?

JAMES. Why would you walk out on me?

JULIE. I don't know. Maybe because you make me really unhappy and it's time to move on. You're the detective. You work it out. Are you sleeping upstairs or are you sleeping down here? I don't mind. Really.

JAMES. I won't be sleeping, Julie!

JULIE. Have you eaten?

JAMES. I can't eat!

JULIE. You should have something. There's that lasagne by the microwave.

JAMES. I never liked lasagne when I wasn't this upset!

JULIE. Fine, fine… just don't…

JAMES. What?

JULIE. Don't go drinking and...

JAMES. What?

JULIE. Waking me up to talk to me. Seriously, James, I need to sleep. I'm wrung out with all this.

JAMES. All what?

JULIE. It'll all start now, won't it? The 'Hate Julie' campaign. I'm the witch, the evil faithless bitch. You've no idea what I'm about to go through. My mother always liked you. She'll never understand this. I'm going to be worn down to a wee stub by you all.

JAMES. You should eat some lasagne. Keep your strength up.

JULIE. No. That's for you. I had some toast and honey. We need more honey.

    JULIE *starts to leave.*

JAMES. Julie?

    She stops.

JULIE. What?

JAMES. Where are you going?

JULIE. Just... I've got somewhere to go.

JAMES. Where?

JULIE. I just want a little peace, James. For a while.

JAMES. Are you...? You're *shagging* some...!?

JULIE (*interrupts*). No! Come to bed. Two months from now you'll be out feeding lager to some divorced WPC, the two of you in matching yellow rain macs. Slagging me off.

    Pause.

JAMES. I'm going to watch a bit of telly.

JULIE. Well, keep the volume down, eh? I'm wrung out to nothing.

JULIE *exits.* JAMES *watches television.*

A nature programme about pandas. JAMES *angrily opens one of the boxes. He thinks it's her stuff for moving out; it's not. He stares into the box for a few moments and then pulls it out – a beautiful rug, a picture of a panda.*

Fade lights into: A pink cherry blossom dawn. Trees laden with spring blossom. A blackbird greeting the light…

Early morning, looking over The Meadows, Edinburgh.

JIE HUI *and* LIN HAN, *a young Chinese man and woman, are sitting watching the early sun. They say the first few sentences in Mandarin then slip into English. But in fact they are still talking in Mandarin throughout the scene.*

LIN HAN. *Wǒ zhī dào nǐ shì bú shì zài shuō huǎng.* [I can tell if you're lying.]

JIE HUI. *Nǐ shuō shí me?* [What do you mean?]

LIN HAN. *Zhè shì tè yì gōng néng. Zhè shì wǒ zuì hǎo de tè yì gōng néng.* [It's magic. It's my best bit of magic.] I can look in someone's face and I know if they're lying or telling the truth. Test me.

Go on.

Tell me something.

JIE HUI. It's really warm. The sun is shining.

LIN HAN. The sun is still rising somewhere behind those weird houses and I can't feel my toes. Any idiot knows that's not true.

Try again.

JIE HUI. I… love my mother.

She studies him for a moment.

LIN HAN. Yes you do.

Go again.

JIE HUI. I love… these chips.

She takes a bag of chips from him.

LIN HAN. No. They've been cold for hours.

Again.

JIE HUI. I love… talking to you.

LIN HAN (*studying him*). No. You don't. That was a lie. That's alright. We've only just met. It's hard work talking to people you don't know.

She looks around.

What is this place?

JIE HUI. It's The Meadows.

LIN HAN. What does that mean, 'Meadows'.

JIE HUI. Like a field… full of flowers.

LIN HAN. Where are the flowers?

JIE HUI. I don't know.

LIN HAN. Never mind. It's a pretty green.

Beat.

I think it's possible.

I think it's possible that I could love you. I think I could fall in love with you. I think this could be a great passion.

JIE HUI *says nothing.*

I'd like to feel a great passion, I'd really like that.

This is the best time in my life for a great passion. Later it would be horrible, if you see someone who's crazy in love and they already have loose skin on their neck that is a sad, sad thing. That's like looking at a crazy person. Some fool that doesn't know she's too old for love. If we're going to fall in love we should do it now. We should do it now sitting under this small sky looking at the sunrise and the cherry trees. This would be a very good time. Sitting in a green field in a strange land looking at the dawn. This is a perfect time.

Let's do it now.

Let's fall in love now.

What do you think?

Pause.

JIE HUI. I think that's… an interesting idea.

LIN HAN. That's not true. You're surprised. Why are you surprised? I told you in my e-mails. I told you that we'd discuss all this.

JIE HUI. I didn't realise we'd discuss it so quickly.

LIN HAN. We've been talking for hours.

Beat.

JIE HUI. Maybe we should see how we get along. Maybe we should remember this is just our first date.

LIN HAN. I have a return flight in two days. There's no time for indecision.

JIE HUI. No.

LIN HAN. We should commit to passion and love… now!

Deep breath.

Like breathing in the scent of those cherry tees.

JIE HUI. They've no smell.

LIN HAN *sniffs dubiously.*

LIN HAN. What's wrong with them?

JIE HUI. They're a different sort of cherry tree.

LIN HAN. They're untidy.

So.

A breath of cold air, that smells of wet grass and cold chips…

Breathes.

And we're in love.

JIE HUI. Just like that?

LIN HAN. Just like that.

Do you feel it?

JIE HUI. No.

Do you?

LIN HAN. No, I'm not going to feel it *first*. I'm not an idiot. I'll wait for you and then I'll feel it. When you look at me with love I'll fill up with your passion and hold it for ever.

JIE HUI. Couldn't we do it the other way round? Couldn't you look at me with love?

LIN HAN. No. You're a man. If we do it the other way round you'll run away. The love in my eyes will terrify you. It's like looking at a great storm sweeping towards you, full of longing and tears. Only a woman could look into the eye of a storm like that and not run away.

JIE HUI. I don't think I can just…

LIN HAN. Come on. Be decisive, choose to love me. Be strong.

JIE HUI *hesitates.*

You're not sure. You think you can do better.

JIE HUI. It's just a bit quick.

LIN HAN. I began writing to you eighteen months ago.

JIE HUI. Yes.

LIN HAN. We have exchanged five hundred and thirty-six e-mails. And seventy-two jpegs.

JIE HUI. Yes.

LIN HAN. You know my favourite colour, my favourite animal and my life's ambition…

JIE HUI. I can't remember your favourite animal.

LIN HAN. It's the panda. Because it lives in my home province but it is adored and protected all over the world. It has achieved my life's ambition to be world famous and loved just for being what it is.

JIE HUI. Yes, I remember.

LIN HAN. How can you forget that? The panda is my symbol. It's on our rugs.

JIE HUI. Yes.

LIN HAN. Yours is the rat because it makes the best of whatever sewer it's born into…

JIE HUI. I was kind of joking…

LIN HAN. So you've had time to talk to me and think about me and consider me in sixty-eight different poses – whereas you only sent me four pictures – but now you think you can do better?

JIE HUI. I'd just like to slow down a bit?

LIN HAN. I'm not a slow person. Love is not a slow emotion.

JIE HUI. It can be. Love can grow very slowly. Like bread rising. Like ice thawing…

LIN HAN. I despise that kind of love.

Of course you can do better than me. There are girls who are prettier than me…

JIE HUI. No, no, I didn't mean…

LIN HAN (*relentless*). There are girls who are much prettier than me, you might even meet one of them. Everywhere you look you can see girls who are prettier than me, more athletic, more intelligent, talented, musical girls who could make you laugh, make you the envy of your friends…

JIE HUI. You're very pretty.

LIN HAN. Thank you. I might not be the prettiest girl you ever meet. I might not even be the prettiest girl you meet who is available to have a relationship and willing to have one with you…

That's your gamble. I'm here, now, I'm quite pretty, quite athletic, quite talented. We're young, but not too young. The timing is good, so you take a chance. I'm a chance. Take me or wait and see if there's something better.

JIE HUI. You're not very romantic are you?

LIN HAN. Yes. I am. The romance comes after. The romance comes after you choose to fill up with a storm of love for me. Then we go crazy with romance. You won't believe how romantic I am. But you have to love me first.

JIE HUI. Just like that?

LIN HAN. Of course.

JIE HUI. You're so old-fashioned.

LIN HAN (*offended*). No. I'm completely modern. I just see things the way they are.

JIE HUI. It's sweet… kind of.

LIN HAN. I'm not sweet.

JIE HUI. I only meant…

LIN HAN (*getting up*). Alright, so I was born in a village, I admit that. But don't say that to me. I see what I see. I'm not lying.

JIE HUI. I never said you were.

Look… I'm very tired.

LIN HAN. I'm not. It's the jet lag. They say you should spend the whole first day in a new country under the sky, not under a roof. Then the sun resets the clock in your head. I'm going to spend the whole day outside. You should go to bed. When you wake up you'll know what to do.

JIE HUI. I can't go to bed. I have a meeting.

LIN HAN. Where is it?

JIE HUI. At our distributor's office.

LIN HAN. Where is that?

JIE HUI. Not far.

LIN HAN. Good. I should be at this meeting.

JIE HUI. No.

LIN HAN. Yes! This man is our client. He is buying my family's rugs. I should see his face.

JIE HUI. It's better… if I meet him alone. Just till the deal is finished.

LIN HAN. You think I will destroy your business? It's my business too. I am very good at business.

JIE HUI. It's just he's used to talking to me…

You can meet him later. Tomorrow.

LIN HAN. Or at the end of your negotiation. How long is your meeting?

JIE HUI. I don't know. Maybe an hour.

LIN HAN. I'll come and find you in an hour. Where? Tell me exactly. I want to know where you'll be.

JIE HUI *points*.

JIE HUI. You see that spire there? That's a church and beside it is the office.

LIN HAN. I can find that. We can go on talking.

JIE HUI. We've been talking all night.

LIN HAN. But you haven't reached a decision. We should go on talking until you have reached a decision. I'll help you.

JIE HUI. Lin Han… it has been very good talking to you. And I don't want you to be unhappy.

LIN HAN. That's good. We want the same thing. We're becoming compatible.

Beat.

JIE HUI. You know nothing about me, not really, I could be anyone! I could be a thief or... a... a killer!

LIN HAN. Are you a killer? Because you should tell me something like that straight away. I wasn't paying attention. Say that again. I'll know if you're lying.

JIE HUI. Look, don't come and meet me. We need this man's money. You won't understand anything. It'll be confusing if we're both there, it'll look bad.

LIN HAN. I won't come for your meeting. I'll come afterwards. In an hour.

JIE HUI. Or I could see you at the hotel. I've a lot to do today. I can't wait around. If I miss you I'll find you at the hotel later.

LIN HAN. You won't miss me. I'll meet you in an hour. There. Where your meeting is. Tell the businessman to expect me at the end of your meeting.

JIE HUI (*sighs impatiently*). I'll see you later then.

He starts to leave.

You're alright? You know where you are?

LIN HAN. Yes. I'm just going to reset my clock.

She turns her face up to the sun. JIE HUI *exits.*

Fade lights into: A huge urban tree looming over, blocking the early sun. An angry rustle of leaves.

Outside ANDY's *office.*

ANDY, *a man in his late thirties/early forties is talking to* JIE HUI.

ANDY (*looking up at the tree*). I hate that tree. It's too dark.

It's not good. Business premises need light, otherwise, subconsciously, people think you've got something to hide.

Plus when the leaves come off you end up sweeping them up the whole time or you've got clients going arse over tit down the basement steps. Wet leaves, lethal. Got to sweep them up but sometimes… given the staffing-to-profit balance I'm currently maintaining… sometimes that means potential business, potential clients, see me with a broom in my hand. Not good. Not an accurate reflection of this business's status.

If it was up to me I'd be at it with a chainsaw but apparently it's council property. I've made complaints.

He looks at his watch.

Want to grab a coffee till we can get in the office?

JIE HUI. You don't have keys?

ANDY. Not with me, no. Hectic morning. Left on the kitchen table. The girl's usually here to open up but it's her day off… Not to worry. Julie'll be along in a minute. She just had to shift some stock.

JIE HUI *looks at his watch.*

Not in a rush are you?

As JIE HUI *doesn't respond:*

You're in a hurry? You have to be somewhere else?

JIE HUI. I have to leave, before the end of the hour. In about half an hour.

ANDY. Oh… right then. Don't know what's keeping her. We'll give her five minutes. Your guys in China still happy with the money deal? All signed up for future orders?

JIE HUI. The owner's daughter has flown here to finalise it.

ANDY. See, you are a smart, smart operator. Balance on arrival in the UK. Brilliant for the cash flow. You didn't tell her we weren't paying customs duty, did you?

JIE HUI. Of course not! They're just very happy with the price we can offer.

ANDY. And I'm happy we can give some of that to them and none of it to Her Majesty's Customs and Bloodsuckers. I was always happy to do that. No victims. No pain. You can't call it crime, can you?

JIE HUI. Andy? What's going on?

ANDY. See, we just need to keep an eye on what's *really* important. And what's the most important thing, in any deal?

JIE HUI. Trust.

ANDY. I was going to say reasonable opportunity for profit, but you're taking us a bit deeper. I like it. Indeed. Trust.

JIE HUI. Why are you moving stock?

ANDY. Oh, just… one of those unexpected… things.

JIE HUI. You've moved my client's stock? Where is it?

ANDY. No, no, it's all fine, it's all safe.

JIE HUI. Where?

ANDY. Julie's completely trustworthy. She's looking after it all personally.

JIE HUI. Why was it moved?

ANDY. Just… a timing issue.

JIE HUI. Which was?

ANDY. Look… I told you I could pull this off and I can. We're fine. I know how to play this. I've no problem taking a customs inspection…

JIE HUI. A customs inspection!? You promised me there would be no complications. You promised us this was safe!

ANDY. They'll be in and out! It'll all be fixed before close of play. My word on it.

JIE HUI. I need payment now. The stock has arrived. We need the money.

ANDY. Yeah, yeah, yeah. I've done this before, man. Just... be cool. Everything's under control.

JIE HUI. Then why are we still standing out here?

ANDY *looks at his watch again.*

ANDY. She'll only be a few minutes.

Trust. Trust. Everything comes down to that, Jie Hui, doesn't it?

I tell you what's going on.

You tell me... Because you didn't exactly give me the full picture, did you, Jie?

JIE HUI. Andy, what's going on?

ANDY *is looking at him searchingly.*

ANDY. You're asking me? You don't know?

JIE HUI. That's why I'm asking you.

ANDY *stares at him for a telling moment, working it out, a big realisation.*

ANDY. Right... right... See, I had you down for a smart boy. An impressive operator. China impressed the hell out of me, Jie Hui. It's staggering what's happening in your bit of the Earth, just... awesome. You've got skyscrapers growing like bamboo. I sat there, when I was last over, I watched the things grow, I mean you could see it, in a day.

A golden tsunami...

I really thought we could surf that thing together, Jie Hui. I did. Never mind. Never mind. You'll get there.

He pats JIE HUI *consolingly.*

You're a good lad. Bright-eyed, bushy-tailed and blinking in the daylight, eh? I'll get us through this. Never you worry.

Trust me.

JIE HUI. About what?

ANDY. Have I told you about my mum?

JIE HUI. Yes.

ANDY. Of course I have. She had to struggle in the dark. She wanted better for me. She wanted me to step into the light. Do you see?

JIE HUI. No.

ANDY. Daylight is expensive. I need one last push, one last wee injection of grubby gold to get me out of the shadows.

Ach, I'm confusing you. Don't worry.

It's just I'm at a crossroads you might say. I've got the hard choices to make now…

JIE HUI. What choices?

ANDY. Well, let me ask you…

Love or money.

Is it a choice?

JIE HUI. You're asking me?

ANDY. It's a question I need answered.

It's a decision I need to make.

Maybe I should make it right now.

He takes a coin out of his pocket and starts to toss it, observing results, making little noises of reaction.

JIE HUI. What are you doing?

ANDY. Trying it out.

JIE HUI. Trying what out?

ANDY. My decision. Accept the woman of my lustful dreams into my soul as well as my bed or…

Tosses the coin.

…ease her back out of my life rapido…

Tosses the coin again.

Right… heads again… like a sign…

JIE HUI. You're deciding to marry…

ANDY. Woah! No! Never that far… She's moved in. Should I move her out?

JIE HUI. You're deciding that on the toss of a coin?

ANDY. Of course not, that would be brutal… Just…

Tosses the coin again.

Seeing how it feels.

It's heads again.

Jeez, will you look at that?

Just… passing the time.

Tosses the coin.

Ah! Had to happen. Well… that might be for the best. Tails.

Dump her. Yes. Try that one again…

Tosses the coin.

JIE HUI. Can we go in?

ANDY. Julie. The key.

Tosses the coin.

And it's bloody heads again!

Well, it can *bring* you money, can't it? Once you've got the right support… the right woman… I have been without the support of the right woman for far far too long. And that's what comes of ignoring your mother and of confusing education and intelligence.

My mother warned me but I wouldn't listen. Madeleine my ex never got it. Truth is, she'd got class but she'd no dress sense and *she* couldny cover my back when business got wobbly.

She didn't even really want to know what the business was… which might have been just as well… but… you know, a bit of concerned interest would have been a nice change.

She thought taxis were a waste of money and Ballachulish is a decent destination for a summer holiday.

How could I make the good life with a woman like that?

How is Susie by the way?

Because you've got yourself a smart girl there.

JIE HUI. Where?

ANDY. Your Susie?

She's a clever cookie. A very smart little biscuit indeed. God, that was some night when you hooked us all up, eh? Some night. How drunk were we? I mean seriously, the whole world turned purple, couldn't talk, could we? Like chewing fog.

JIE HUI. We were very drunk.

ANDY. We were very very drunk.

How tall is Susie if you don't mind me asking?

JIE HUI. How tall?

ANDY. Yeah, if it's not a rude question.

JIE HUI. About one metre eighty.

ANDY. So that's what? Five foot eleven.

Wow. *Wow!* I thought it was just the heels. Where's she from?

JIE HUI. Montrose.

ANDY. Really. I thought she was Swedish. She speaks really clear English… I mean, for someone from Montrose. Did you meet her brothers before you started going out?

JIE HUI. On our second date.

ANDY (*laughs*). You're a brave man shagging their sister. I tell you, those boys would even frighten my mum.

JIE HUI. But they've been good for us. For our business.

ANDY. If you say so. As long as they're happy. Are they happy?

JIE HUI (*shrugs*). They got the shipping contract. Why wouldn't they be happy?

ANDY. Good, good, good. So we don't need to be telling them about any customs bother...

JIE HUI. You said there was no problem.

ANDY. *Absolutely* no problem.

Tosses the coin.

You know there's a definite bias to the true-love pattern here. So. You and Susie. Going well, is it? Good communication? Plenty of trust?

JIE HUI. We've split up.

ANDY. When did that happen?

JIE HUI. That night.

ANDY. That *night*? Why? What...?

JIE HUI. We were very drunk.

ANDY. Aw, fuck, she'll get over that. Give her another week.

JIE HUI. No. It's over.

ANDY. No way. She was all over you.

JIE HUI. I was sick in her bed.

ANDY (*laughing*). Aw, man, that is bad. Yeah okay, serious dog-house time, I get it but...

JIE HUI. She won't forgive that. It was unforgiveable.

ANDY. Thing is, man... between you and me, you might be better off out of the whole thing.

JIE HUI. I'll never find another woman like Susie.

ANDY. No. Right enough.

Sorry.

This is turning into quite a day. Quite a day.

Julie just turned up on the doorstep, first thing this morning.

She's left him. I've got her. She's mine. I won.

I won.

Or did I? What do you think? She's worth it, isn't she?

JIE HUI. Who?

ANDY. You met her that night. My little Julie... (*Thinks*.)

That woman has a mind like a money-seeking missile, I tell you, she could find a venture-capital opportunity under a bit of camel dung at the arse end of the Gobi Desert. She was the one saw those rugs would be sellers. 'An eye for marketable beauty,' that's what she says to me, 'I've an eye for marketable beauty.' I says, 'What other kind of beautiful's worth having...'

JIE HUI. What time is she getting here?

ANDY. She's a looker, isn't she? No doubt about it...

But... on the one hand I tell her to take the sample boxes somewhere safe and she dumps them in the front room she shares with Mr Plod the policeman. And then she just leaves them there...

JIE HUI. What!?

ANDY. It's fine. It's all fine. It's already sorted. She's picking them up in the van as we speak...

We had words about it.

You see, there it is. We had words. Do I want domestics in the middle of my downtime? Jie Hui, I need peace. Some-where in my life I need a little haven of peace!

Fuck, I do want her, though. We're having the row. I go out the room… cool down… come back in… she's only gone to sleep. Cat-napping in my leather chair, little stockinged feet tucked up under her cute little arse.

Fucking adorable.

Sweet as you like, but is she good for business? The way my business is right now…?

Maybe I should stick her in a hotel for a bit, just till we see how we go. I mean, if she's in my *house*…

JIE HUI. What?

ANDY. Could all go tits-up, couldn't it?… Aye, maybe should just stick her in that empty rental I've got in Meadowbank… just till we see… What do you think?

JIE HUI. I think if we don't get into your office to get my client's money now I'm leaving and you have no deal.

ANDY *sighs*.

ANDY. I'll get in the bathroom window.

The window is head height above them on the wall. ANDY *considers it a moment.*

Don't suppose you could give me a boost-up?

JIE HUI *just looks at him.* ANDY *climbs up and starts trying to get in the window.*

(*Breathless.*) There'll be alarms going off when I do this unless I can get them switched off in time, you know.

He might get as far as being head first, arse out the window. He might only be scrambling up the wall but, at whatever moment works, there's a dull shot.

ANDY *jerks and slides down the wall.*

JIE HUI *stares at him for a moment, shocked. Then he tentatively crosses to* ANDY*'s slumped body.*

JIE HUI. Andy? Andy?

He checks ANDY*'s pulse, straightens up, still at a loss, in shock. Swears in Mandarin. He takes his phone out.*

LIN HAN *enters, again, they speak their first few lines in Mandarin before continuing in English.*

LIN HAN. *Fā shēng shí me shì le?* [What's happened?]

JIE HUI. *Méi shì, bié huāng.* [It's alright. Don't panic.]

(*Into phone in English.*) Hullo? Yes, I need an ambulance…

LIN HAN (*panicking*). *Fā shēng shí me le? Nǐ gàn le shí me?* [What's happened!? What have you done?]

JIE HUI.…Four Buccleuch Close. Round the back, off the little car park at the back, off the street.

(*To* LIN HAN.) Don't be stupid. I didn't do this.

(*Into phone.*) I don't know. I think maybe he was shot. I don't know just…

LIN HAN (*screaming over this*). What did you do!?

JIE HUI (*cutting call*).…get here, okay!

(*Moving in on* LIN HAN.) Look, Lin Han, calm down, come away from him, come over here. Calm down. I didn't do this.

LIN HAN. Look in my eyes and say that.

JIE HUI. Lin Han, you're a little bit crazy. You're a little bit crazy and I don't want to fall in love with you, so go back to the hotel.

LIN HAN. You said you could be a killer.

JIE HUI. You're a crazy woman.

Look, Lin Han, the truth is I have a girlfriend, her name is Susie, she's very tall and very beautiful and she's almost Swedish. We're very much in love and I'm going to marry her. Understand?

And I don't kill people.

LIN HAN. You're lying! You just told me a lie! I know! I can see! I can always see!

LIN HAN backs off.

JIE HUI. Lin Han…

LIN HAN. Liar! Killer!

LIN HAN runs off.

JIE HUI. Lin Han!

He runs after her.

Fade lights into: The tree tossing angrily in sudden high wind, a surge of wind in the branches…

Police station interview room.

MADELEINE, *a forty-something woman, sits opposite* JAMES.

JAMES. Alright?

MADELEINE. Yes.

JAMES. Comfortable enough?

MADELEINE. Lovely, thank you.

Pause.

It's a bit warm.

JAMES. Aye, sorry, no control over that. Take a layer off if you like.

MADELEINE. No, no… it's eh… I'm fine.

Thank you.

She looks around.

So. This is where it all happens.

JAMES. All what?

MADELEINE (*thrown*). I don't know… police stuff.

JAMES. Aye. Some of it.

Awkward pause.

So what is it you do yourself?

MADELEINE. Oh… well… the easiest way to explain it is I study wee beasties. The really tiny ones.

JAMES. Plankton?

MADELEINE. No. Fleas then. I study fleas. That's the simple way to describe it. Completely inaccurate but…

JAMES. That's not what you do?

MADELEINE. Not precisely no, not at all really, but that's what…

JAMES. So what do you do?

MADELEINE. I'm a biologist. An entomologist.

I specialise in lice.

JAMES. Head lice?

MADELEINE. Fur lice. Or the kinds of lice, some kinds of lice, that you find on long-haired mammals.

Specifically I'm looking at the fur lice of endangered species.

Specifically I'm studying one type of louse that tends to be found in the fur of giant pandas.

In the wild. Not in zoos. They don't have them in the zoos.

That's sort of the point.

JAMES. What is?

MADELEINE. If the wild panda becomes extinct so do its lice.

JAMES. And that would be bad because…?

MADELEINE. It's called biodiversity.

JAMES. Is it now.

MADELEINE. It means…

JAMES. I know what it means.

Beat.

Why did you no just say you were an entomologist?

MADELEINE. I say I study wee beasties. I've learned that's for the best.

JAMES *scratches his head, looking over his notes.*

See, you're doing it.

JAMES. What?

MADELEINE. Scratching. You won't be able to stop now. Talking about fleas makes folk scratch a bit. Talking about lice gets them tearing their scalp off. Wee beasties. Kinder to everyone.

Sorry.

Beat.

So… what's this about?

JAMES. We're waiting on my colleague.

MADELEINE. Oh?

JAMES. Needs to be two of us.

MADELEINE. Oh right! And then you switch the tape on and we…

JAMES. There you go, then that's all proper.

MADELEINE. So you were just…?

JAMES. Talking to you. Making conversation. Small talk.

MADELEINE. Oh shit! Sorry. I thought we were…

JAMES. No.

MADELEINE. Sorry.

Beat. JAMES *scratches again.*

I'm sorry.

JAMES. Don't worry about it.

MADELEINE. No really…

JAMES (*slightly tetchy*). No really. Don't worry about it.

MADELEINE. Did you have them when you were a kid?

JAMES. What?

MADELEINE. Because that makes it worse, if you actually remember…

JAMES (*interrupts*). You're asking if I had nits?

MADELEINE. Nothing to be ashamed of.

I did.

They prefer clean hair, you know.

JAMES. No. I did not have nits.

MADELEINE. Plenty do.

JAMES gets up and looks out the door.

Is this an interview room?

JAMES. Yes.

MADELEINE. So am I…?

JAMES. What?

MADELEINE. I'm not under arrest or anything?

JAMES. No.

MADELEINE. This is just how you do it.

JAMES. Yes. This is how we do it. Only ideally there needs to be two of us.

Impatient, JAMES exits the interview room, slamming the door behind him with an almighty crash.

MADELEINE *jumps.*

After a nervous moment she gets up and slowly walks to the door. Fearing the worst she tries to open it. It opens.

JAMES is standing right outside.

MADELEINE. Oh Jesus! Sorry…

JAMES. Bathroom?

MADELEINE. Sorry?

JAMES. Down that way. Bit of a state at the minute, mind…

MADELEINE. No, I just thought…

No, I'm fine.

JAMES moves back in and sets up some recording equipment, tired, impatient.

JAMES. Well, no bugger's coming, are they?

Sorry.

We're short-handed. Report of gunfire in Pilton.

MADELEINE. God.

JAMES. Aye. Good night to be inside. Looks like rain too.

Alright, it's not ideal but let's get on.

MADELEINE. We're starting?

JAMES. We're starting.

MADELEINE. Just… us?

As JAMES doesn't answer:

Don't there need to be two of you then?

Beat.

JAMES. I'll try and cope.

MADELEINE. If you were going to arrest me would there have to be two of you?

JAMES. Why would we arrest you?

MADELEINE. No reason… just… general… guilt. Everyone feels guilty, don't they; at some level, everyone *is* guilty… aren't they? At some level.

JAMES. Probably.

So. Do you know a man called Andy Telfer?

MADELEINE. Yes.

I'm sorry about the lice thing. Really. I'd hate for you to think of me as the lice lady. That's not who I am.

Pause.

JAMES. Okay.

So, what's your relationship to Mr Telfer?

MADELEINE. We were a couple. For six years.

JAMES. And when was the last time you saw him?

MADELEINE. To talk to?

JAMES. What?

MADELEINE. When was the last time I saw him to talk to? About a year ago.

JAMES. And when was the last time you saw him?

MADELEINE. What's happened to him? Is he alright?

JAMES. Miss Murray...

MADELEINE. Dr Murray...

JAMES. Dr Murray, could you answer the question, please.

Pause.

Are you refusing to answer the question?

MADELEINE. I've forgotten the question.

JAMES. When was the last time you saw Andy Telfer?

Pause.

MADELEINE. A year ago in June. He came to get the last of his CDs.

JAMES. And that was the last time you saw him.

A small hesitation.

MADELEINE. Yes.

JAMES. When was the last time you were in the vicinity of his office?

MADELEINE. This morning.

JAMES. This morning?

MADELEINE. I walk up his street to get across to my office at the university.

JAMES. Every morning?

MADELEINE. Every morning.

JAMES. So did you see him?

MADELEINE. I never see him.

JAMES. Never?

MADELEINE. I know what time he goes in to work.

JAMES. And you avoid him.

MADELEINE. I avoid him.

JAMES. Must be a bit awkward. Why don't you just walk up the next street over?

MADELEINE. Why the fuck should I?! He left me. Why does *my* life have to get rearranged?!

A moment between them.

Sorry, I didn't mean to… swear like that, I…

JAMES. No, you're alright.

Another moment.

MADELEINE. Can I…? Can I have a drink of water, please?

JAMES gets her some water. He hands it to her. He's watching her closely. She takes a drink, looking back at him.

It's another moment, they're noticing each other.

Thanks.

JAMES. No problem.

MADELEINE. So what's happened to him?

JAMES. He's been attacked.

Pause.

MADELEINE. And how is he?

JAMES. It's touch and go at the moment.

Pause.

MADELEINE. I see.

Shit.

Okay.

Was he… Was he… asking for me?

JAMES. He hasn't regained consciousness.

MADELEINE. I see.

So… how did you know about me?

JAMES. We asked, at his office.

MADELEINE. Yes.

JAMES. They had your contact details.

MADELEINE. Right.

JAMES. His secretary said she saw you on the street most mornings.

MADELEINE. Right.

Well, I told you about that. I was there most mornings.

JAMES. On your way to teach your Honours student tutorial? Between nine and twelve-fifteen?

MADELEINE. Yes… how did you…?

JAMES. We checked.

JAMES *is reading notes.*

Mr Telfer runs an import business.

MADELEINE (*sighs*). Oh, he does all sorts of things.

JAMES. From China.

JAMES *is finally absorbing the information he is reading.*

MADELEINE. Oh, he's gone with that, has he?

That's my fault, I'm afraid.

JAMES. Your fault?

MADELEINE. I finally persuaded him to come on one of my study trips.

He hated it, of course...

JAMES. Hated what?

MADELEINE. The spitting, the staring and the plumbing. That about summed it up, I think. Though most of the time he was laid up in the hotel room. That was a 'shit hole', of course. The whole place was a shit hole apparently. The plumbing literally was a shit hole so...

Rural China, not Beijing. He liked Beijing.

There are few countries in the world that understand the British and American obsession with invisible plumbing. They do all these amazing things to open up to tourism but they can't get their heads round the notion that we're so pathologically terrified by any prolonged vision of our own shit we'll pass up the chance to visit all of the world's wonders unless they have flushing toilets attached. Anyway. You don't want to know all that.

JAMES (*reading*). Shit!

MADELEINE. What?

JAMES. His business.

MADELEINE. Oh yeah. He came up with this scheme to start importing Chinese crafts, smaller stuff you know, like... rugs...

JAMES. With pandas on them?

MADELEINE. I couldn't tell you.

Sounds about right. Probably a bit more to it, of course.

Probably something very lucrative.

MADELEINE *is clearly upset.*

JAMES. Were you aware of any… irregularities in his business finances?

MADELEINE. Oh, I don't think he's *dodgy*… Is he?

JAMES. Customs says he is.

MADELEINE. I don't know anything about that. Seriously. I just…

She's clearly upset.

JAMES. What is it, Dr Murray?

MADELEINE. He doesn't give a fuck about pandas! How dare he?! How dare he, of all people. You know what he used to say? 'What's the point in pandas? You can't eat them, you can't make a coat out of them and you can't watch them shagging. Give me rabbits any day,' he said. *Arse*hole!

JAMES. That's what he said?

MADELEINE. All the time. He liked… winding me up.

It was foreplay once, of course.

JAMES. He wound you up?

MADELEINE. In every way.

You can make a coat out of a panda as it happens. There are some sick, fabulously wealthy freaks out there secretly stroking poached, panda-pelt jackets. Like hanging a stolen Manet in a locked cellar. Money they can't show anyone but they still want it.

I bet he's got child labourers knitting fake-fur coats and calling it panda. Sort of thing he would do. Sort of thing I was stupid enough to tolerate in the name of true love.

Idiot!

JAMES. You sound pretty angry, Dr Murray.

MADELEINE. Have you ever gone through a major relationship split?

JAMES *says nothing*.

Believe me, for one year in, I'm doing really well.

JAMES. You're still angry.

MADELEINE. Only if I talk about it.

But I suppose we can't change the subject. In the circumstances.

It turned out he was two-timing me, you know. For six months. In his head that's probably my fault, I refused to fall out of love with him within his timetable.

JAMES. Who was he two-timing you with?

MADELEINE. I don't know who she is... some... bimbette rug importer probably.

Pause.

JAMES. For six months. He was sleeping with this other woman for six months?

MADELEINE. Just over.

JAMES. So he's been with her a year.

MADELEINE. Eighteen months. Six months of two-timing. A year of presumably monogamous bliss.

JAMES. Jesus...

MADELEINE. I know. What I have to tell myself is that it doesn't make me a clown. That my naivety... my trust... was still something beautiful.

JAMES. You think?

MADELEINE. Of course. But *believing* that I'm not actually a
naive, trusting reject from a Disney cartoon… that takes work.

Beat.

Look… I'm sorry. I know. It's deeply unattractive.

JAMES. What?

MADELEINE. Sad old women raging about their ex-partners.

JAMES. You're not old.

And you're not unattractive.

MADELEINE (*surprised*). Thank you.

JAMES. So. He's an arse.

MADELEINE. He's dying? Is that what you're telling me? He's
dying?

JAMES. They don't know.

MADELEINE. But…

JAMES. What?

MADELEINE. He was shot?

JAMES. Did I say that?

MADELEINE (*thrown*). Didn't you say that?

JAMES (*smiles*). Need to check the tape.

Pause.

MADELEINE. I really have to catch this flight, you know.

JAMES. We might have to ask you to rearrange that.

MADELEINE. I don't know if I can…

JAMES. Travel insurance'll cover it.

MADELEINE. But why? Just ask me whatever you need to ask
me. How long can that take?

JAMES. Well, it might take me a bit longer for me to know what I need to ask you.

So why did you think Mr Telfer had been shot?

Pause.

MADELEINE. Recently I've been hoping someone might shoot him.

Or run him over. Was he run over?

JAMES. No. He was shot.

MADELEINE. Oh.

JAMES. And you're not very upset about it.

MADELEINE. I'm not.

Or maybe I am.

I'm confused.

Should I be upset?

JAMES *says nothing.*

Can I ask you something?

Do you think I look like I wear a fleece?

JAMES. A fleece?

MADELEINE. You know those neat little all-purpose, all-weather, long-sleeved fleeces. So practical. You buy them out of Sunday supplements.

JAMES. I'm not following.

MADELEINE. Or do you think I might be dangerous?

Pause.

JAMES. Dangerous in what sense?

Pause.

MADELEINE. Am I allowed to touch you?

JAMES. Excuse me?

MADELEINE. Is that…?

She looks towards the recording equipment.

Okay then…

Without saying anything else, she gets up and crosses to JAMES. She pauses, her face close to his, he doesn't move. She kisses him, gently at first, then as he responds, with real passion.

She breaks away. She goes back and sits down again. Exactly as before.

Okay then…

Ask me whatever you like.

JAMES (*shaken*). Right…

MADELEINE. Okay?

JAMES. Okay, please… please don't do that again.

MADELEINE. Are you sure?

Pause.

JAMES. Why were you talking about fleeces?

MADELEINE. I wear them at work. They're a practical solution to both Scottish weather and cold, wet bamboo forests. They don't define me.

JAMES. Mr Telfer said you were defined by wearing fleeces.

MADELEINE. He implied as much. As I aged, as my work developed. He saw the fleece. Not the woman.

JAMES. So you fancied shooting him?

MADELEINE. You're asking me if I shot Andy Telfer?

JAMES. No. I know you didn't.

MADELEINE. You know I didn't? How?

JAMES. You have an alibi for the time frame and you're not the type.

MADELEINE. Not the type. Right.

Beat.

Okay, well, there is something I should tell you.

There's the sound of voices offstage: a desk sergeant saying, 'Calm down,' etc. and LIN HAN *in a stream of agitated Mandarin, rising in volume over the desk sergeant's attempts to calm her.*

JAMES. What the...?

(*Sighs.*) Excuse me.

JAMES *exits.*

Alone in the room, MADELEINE *checks that the equipment is still recording.*

MADELEINE. This is after you've left the room. Obviously.

I have never in my life felt so... There's not a word that doesn't just sound grubby.

Electric. I feel electric. Charged. Could you feel it?

Once you start giving in to impulses, where does it end? It's got to end. You can't be a runaway truck. You have to take some responsibility.

I have to go back to the bamboo forests, and the mist... just once.

Detective Sergeant...

I'm really sorry. I've forgotten your name.

I'm really sorry, I can't say this to your face.

Detective Sergeant. I would really like to have hot sex with you on this interview table.

Which won't be entirely a surprise after what I just...

I don't actually know what's going on.

I do have a very private recurring fantasy about being strip-searched following a minor traffic violation. But that's with an American policeman who wears mirror shades and calls me ma'am.

I did like it that you hadn't shaved. That was in the fantasy but otherwise…

I just think you're absolutely heart-stoppingly gorgeous.

None of that is what I should be thinking about but that's all I am thinking about.

But I am extremely angry with you.

I am extremely angry with you and I need you to know something.

The door opens and JAMES *puts his head in.*

JAMES. You speak Chinese?

MADELEINE. Eh… a little Mandarin, yes. I can get by.

JAMES. Right.

The door closes again. MADELEINE *waits, uncertain.*

The door opens again and JAMES *ushers* LIN HAN *into the room.* LIN HAN *has clearly been crying.*

JAMES. This is Wang Lin Han.

(*To* LIN HAN.) This is Dr Murray. She can translate.

(*To* MADELEINE.) Lin Han has some information about the attack on Mr Telfer.

MADELEINE. But… don't you have proper translators?

JAMES. Given notice. Aye.

MADELEINE. But…

JAMES (*interrupts*). I'm in a hurry here, alright? Customs boys breathing down my neck and those guys can rip your floor-boards without so much as a 'Can I come in, here's the search warrant.' I need to know what's going on. Who's involved. I need you to ask her!

So ask her!

MADELEINE *speaks to* LIN HAN. *As before, they say the first couple of sentences in Mandarin and then speak in English.*

MADELEINE. *Nǐ hǎo, wǒ shì Murray bó shì, hěn gāo xìng rèn shí nǐ.* [Hullo, I'm Dr Murray, how are you?]

LIN HAN. *Xìng huì.* [Good, thank you. How are you?]

MADELEINE. You have some information about the attack on Mr Telfer?

LIN HAN. Yes.

MADELEINE. Can you tell me what it is?

LIN HAN. I know the man who did this.

Pause.

MADELEINE. Right.

JAMES. What's she saying?

MADELEINE. She has information.

JAMES. Ask her then.

LIN HAN (*rapidly*). I know this man, I know him, he's a liar and a violent man. I should have realised. I should have seen it on his face. But he only sent me four pictures. I stared at his face on my screen and he wasn't lying then! He wasn't! He was a man who could love me...

JAMES. What's she saying?

MADELEINE. I can't...

(*To* LIN HAN.) Slow down, slow down, please.

LIN HAN. I have to tell the police. I have to tell them what he's done.

MADELEINE. This man is a policeman. Tell me and I'll tell him.

LIN HAN *takes a deep breath, composing herself.*

LIN HAN. I am Wang Lin Han. I am nineteen years old. I am here as a representative of the Panda Joy rug company. This is my passport. This is my visa.

She pushes these at MADELEINE.

MADELEINE *looks at them uncertainly, then offers them to* JAMES.

I'm sorry. My English is very good but I'm upset.

MADELEINE. That's alright.

LIN HAN. I'm very upset and I can't think of the words.

MADELEINE. It's okay. Just go slowly.

LIN HAN. I am our company's international representative. Because of my language skills.

MADELEINE. Yes.

LIN HAN. I have been in communication with the representative of a distribution company. He finds contacts and investors to distribute the products of small-scale Chinese manufacturing companies into Europe.

JAMES. What's she saying?

MADELEINE. Nothing yet.

LIN HAN. Sometimes I wrote to this man in our language and sometimes we wrote in English, to practise. We had a very... happy correspondence, we made each other smile... at least... he put smilies in his messages too. So after a few months my father made a joke. He said this man would be the perfect husband for me because it would be so good for the family business. You see my father and my mother would like me to marry very soon but they know I think I shouldn't get married before I'm thirty. So they say things like that, as if they're joking, but I know they mean it too.

JAMES. What's she…?

MADELEINE. I'm not getting all of it.

JAMES. But what…?

MADELEINE. Shoosht, she's getting to the good bit.

LIN HAN. So I stopped the messages with the smilies in them. It was all business. And then he sent me another message with sad faces, and he asked if I was angry with him…

MADELEINE. And you changed your mind?

LIN HAN. Yes! I thought, I've studied English for so long because I wanted to travel. And here I was just working in the same little factory I grew up in, in the same little town. I thought, this man could help me travel. It *would* be great for business so my mum and dad would be happy, I could escape without anyone crying about it.

And I've been in love and it was really horrible. It's really horrible to want someone and be in their power like that.

MADELEINE. Yes.

LIN HAN. So… I thought I should think about a relationship with this man. It would be a practical choice. It would get me what I want. I asked him to send me a picture.

MADELEINE. Yes?

JAMES. What…?

MADELEINE. Shooosh!

(*To* LIN HAN.) Go on.

LIN HAN. It was a beautiful picture. I loved his picture.

MADELEINE. Oh.

LIN HAN. And it wasn't a studio picture! It wasn't lit and air brushed and all shined up in Photoshop. It was just a casual picture. He was on the beach. He was smiling at me with such a look…

MADELEINE. You liked him.

LIN HAN. I fell in love with his picture. I have to be honest
now. I hoped he would love me first but that's what
happened. I fell in love with a picture and a set of letters.
Like a crazy girl who doesn't know what's real.

MADELEINE. That's not crazy, that's…

LIN HAN. Of course it is!

He was right. He was right, I know nothing about him. And
now I love him. Do you know the story about the baby ducks?

JAMES. What's she talking about?

MADELEINE. Baby ducks. Shhh!

LIN HAN. The first thing a baby duck sees moving when it
breaks through its shell it will love as its mother. You can
make them love cats that want to eat them or chase after
bicycle wheels and die in the road. I was just breaking out
into the world. I'm a baby duck and I'm following a killer.

MADELEINE. You don't know that.

LIN HAN. I saw him with the body of this man. He said it had
nothing to do with him, he was talking and talking and I
looked in his eyes and I saw a lie.

Now I've realised I'm a stupid little duckling with shell in
my baby feathers. I've stepped out into the world and it'll
squash me. I thought I knew how to do anything but I'm just
a stupid little girl.

MADELEINE. You can't help who you love.

LIN HAN. No. That's true.

MADELEINE. It doesn't make you stupid, to love someone.

LIN HAN. Yes, it does but it can't be helped.

MADELEINE. No.

LIN HAN. And I really do love him. Even though he probably
is a killer and a liar.

MADELEINE. He might not be.

LIN HAN. He is.

MADELEINE. You should hear his side of it. If you love him.

LIN HAN. You think so?

MADELEINE. You owe it to yourself.

Pause. LIN HAN *is thinking.*

JAMES. Are you going to tell me...?

MADELEINE. Wait! *Wait!*

LIN HAN. You're right. I shouldn't give up so easily.

MADELEINE. There you go.

LIN HAN. And if he really is a killer I might still love him so I should think about what that means.

MADELEINE. I think so.

LIN HAN. Because I can't just betray him. That would be betraying a great love.

MADELEINE. You'd only hurt yourself.

LIN HAN. Yes.

But what about the poor dead man and all the people who love him?

MADELEINE. He's not dead yet. He's in hospital. He's not dead.

Plus he's a bit of an arse.

LIN HAN. Oh.

(*Thinks.*) Then I should wait. I should think about this more carefully.

MADELEINE. That'd be my advice.

LIN HAN. Alright. Thank you.

She looks at JAMES *and smiles at him as she takes back her passport and papers.*

(*In English.*) Thank you very much.

She exits.

JAMES. Where's she off to? What did she say?

MADELEINE. She is convinced the man she has decided to love attacked Andy Telfer.

JAMES. Okay! Name? Current location?

MADELEINE. She's realised that if she truly loves him she can never betray him so she might carry that secret to her grave.

Pause.

JAMES. Aw nice work, thanks a bunch.

He runs after LIN HAN.

Oi, Miss Han! Hold on a minute!

MADELEINE *is alone again. She hesitates then speaks into the recording equipment again.*

MADELEINE. Alright, you listen now! I am dangerous! I am the type! I shot Andy Telfer because he let his arse get fat.

The alibi is pants. Of course I'm marked down as teaching that class but, come on, a tutorial for Honours students at nine-fifteen? There's only three of them and they never show up till eleven.

I was at Andy's work. With my air gun. I shot him. I've always had this idea I wanted to be dangerous. But nothing in my life is really dangerous. So I had Andy. He wasn't a safe choice for a studious entomologist. I loved that.

Andy could sell you anything. He sold me 'forever after' and 'undying love'. It was a hard sell but I bought it in the end.

He used to call me 'Dr Murray' and we'd both get off on that. I was the sleek sexy scientist and he was the dodgy double-dealer. He was a tricky proposition for anyone…

except me. I loved that. I could even cope with his monstrous mother. I was happy.

And as the happy years slipped by he'd never eat his greens or rein in the good times... so he got a bit... wider... and a bit thinner on top... I didn't mind. I'd say, 'I don't mind, I still think you're sexy,' and I'd mean it!

I'm sorry, this probably seems beside the point but what I'm trying to explain is what drove me to shoot Andy in the arse and the fatness of the arse was crucial.

I can forgive the double-dealing, the broken promises, the basic dishonesty... I can't forgive the arse.

Oh, I forgave the fat arse when the man who sat upon it *loved* me! I forgave it completely.

Now that makes me a mug who put up with a two-timing fat arse. The arse itself, the fat arse, is the symbol of the injury. The fact that its owner had no shame about parading that arse around looking for younger, prettier women to grip it in the throes of passion says it all. I was a mug to settle for the fat arse. All women are mugs if they tolerate a fat arse without the sweetener of undying love. The compromises and the compassion of true love, the loving gaze that forgives wobbling buttocks because love is deeper than shallow aesthetics... are all revealed as symptoms of idiocy when he wobbles off with another.

If I had known the arse was going to leave me I would have declared it. I would have just said it. 'Your arse is too fat. Fix it!'

Now obviously you've got... well, you've got a fabulous arse, Detective, if you don't mind me mentioning it, but you know, I can see the rest of you's had some wear and tear and quite frankly... I think that's sexy. So, I am not unreasonable. I'm not demanding Brad Pitt here.

And I think you can see that *I'm* sexy. Whatever I wear.

But when Andy was leaving... he made quite a casual... quite a *cruel* remark, about the fleeces.

He said, 'Anyway, now you can get together with one of those Open University guys with the beards. You can go hill walking in matching fleeces.'

Now I've admitted I do wear a fleece professionally, Detective, but I am not a fleecy woman. How dare he, this man who had literally seen and touched all my intimate openings, how *dare* he call me fleecy?! I might wear a fleece, you bastard, but I can take it off! Where are you going to hang up your fat arse!

He couldn't forgive the fleece.

I *constantly* forgave the fat arse.

That is the source of my murderous rage.

Because I *am* dangerous, Detective.

I realised I had to reinvent myself or wither away to fleecy, smiling nothing. I bought an air gun. I trained for weeks on a shooting range.

There is a tree tucked round the side of a building overlooking the car park at the back of his office, overlooking the main entrance to his work.

There's a branch about halfway up with a clear view of the door. When the tree's in leaf a sniper is invisible lying on that branch... and I wore a camouflage fleece.

I'm leaving for China. For three months.

This morning I loaded my air rifle. I climbed that tree, I lay in wait and when I had a clear shot I gave Andy a bullet in the arse.

I thought he'd feel it.

I had no idea he'd...

Detective, I'm sorry. While we were talking I actually had a fantasy of telling you all this while licking the post-coital sweat from your chest.

I don't recognise the person I've become. I suspect I'll only regret her birth when I hear the cell door closing on me.

Before that happens I have to smell woodsmoke and green bamboo and watch black and white ghost bears moving down the mountainside one more time...

I won't lie to you. If I can escape, I will, but I will be very easy to find.

MADELEINE *hesitates one more moment.*

She peeks out the door, checking out the escape. Relief, all clear.

I hope it's you that finds me.

MADELEINE *exits.*

Fade lights into: Green bamboo forest. Again, very distant... we hear the bleating call of the giant panda.

End of Act One.

ACT TWO

A hospital room.

JULIE *is sitting by the bed, holding* ANDY*'s hand. Or at least she's holding the hand of something that looks like* ANDY. ANDY *himself is standing, looking at his own body. Neither* JULIE *nor, later on in the scene,* JAMES *can hear* ANDY *at any point.*

ANDY. Aw no, this isn't good, is it?

This isn't good.

Outside your body looking at your body.

Never good.

I'm not fucking walking into the light, by the way, so just…

I hear any angel voices I'm stopping right here. Hold on, Andy, hold on…

What can you hold onto? There you go…

Grabs onto bedhead.

See, if the boy with the scythe comes at me? He'll have to cut my arm off.

Oh fuck, I'm scared, oh fuck, I'm scared, oh fuck, I'm…

No I'm not, no I'm not, no I'm not…

Last thoughts.

No, not last thoughts! Ongoing thinking… at a stressful time…

Peering at JULIE.

Is she crying?

Why isn't she crying? Does that mean I'm not dying? Does that mean she doesn't love me?

On the one hand there's no tunnel leading into the light...

On the other I am looking at my own body.

Aw, Mummy, help me!

Aw, get a grip, Andy!

Why's Mum not here? I'm sick! Your mum's supposed to be there when you're sick...

Always had to be really fucking sick before she'd stay off work though, eh?

Remember that? Riding about on the paper round in a T-shirt in February, trying to catch pneumonia so we'd both get a holiday... God, I remember that...

Aw, Jesus, my past life's flashing in front of my eyes! I am dying.

No! If you were dying, Mum would be here!

You think?

Of course!

I don't know... she might have too much on. You know what she's like.

She'd be here if you were dying!

You think?

She'd leave the business to look after itself for five minutes if you were *dying*.

Aye, it'd depend what'd come up though, eh?

Right enough.

And think about it, she wouldny let you lie around in bed if you weren't really sick, would she?

No. She'd tip me out on the floor. 'Shift yourself, you lazy wee bastard. Think you can lie around all day like that damp sack of farts and whisky that calls itself your father?' She had it all to do. Taught me to graft like her. I'm like her now. I never lie down.

Andy, you're definitely lying down now.

Jesus, I must be dying! Where's my mum?

Never mind, Julie's here. Julie? Julie? I love you, darling. Truly I do.

Say I'm not going to die and leave you.

Enter JAMES.

What's he doing here?

JULIE (*looks up and sees* JAMES). Oh.

JAMES. Hi there.

ANDY. Make him go away, Julie.

JULIE. You're not surprised.

JAMES. I'm a detective.

JULIE. It's not like you think.

JAMES. I think you've been two-timing me with an importer of Chinese rugs.

Pause.

JULIE. It's not two-timing if you're in love.

JAMES. Yes it fucking is.

JULIE. It doesn't feel like it.

JAMES. No. No, that's a tough one.

So, you're in love with the victim, are you?

ANDY. You heard her.

JULIE. Victim?

JAMES. I'm not that good a detective. That's why I'm here. He was shot in the arse.

JULIE. They told me it was a heart attack!

ANDY. Jesus, I've had a heart attack!

JAMES. Shock of being shot.

ANDY. I'm too young to have a heart attack!

JAMES. So... you love him.

JULIE. I don't know.

Doesn't look like he's in there.

ANDY. I'm right here!

JULIE. I didn't know there was anything wrong with his heart.

JAMES. Maybe you wore it out.

JULIE. Don't.

JAMES. What?

JULIE. We were finished anyway. I was doing us a favour.

JAMES. For eighteen months.

JULIE. How'd you know that?

JAMES. Sources.

ANDY. How'd he know that?

JULIE. Look... It wasn't easy. I had to be really strong.

JAMES. I bet.

ANDY. Julie? What else does he know?

JULIE. I couldn't just come out and tell you I'd met someone.

You'd've been raging.

JAMES. Oh, right enough, it's so much better to find out this way.

JULIE. Actually I couldn't tell you anything, James! Ever!

JAMES. Don't remember you trying that hard.

JULIE. Where do I work, James?

JAMES. You think I don't know that?!

JULIE. I started working with Andy eighteen months ago.

JAMES. Did you tell me?

JULIE. Yes.

JAMES. What did I say?

JULIE. 'That'll be nice for you.'

ANDY. And it was.

JULIE. And I tried to tell you we were in trouble. The night I told you how much I loved my willow-pattern tea set…

ANDY. We love willow-pattern!

JAMES is just looking blank.

JULIE.…and you don't even remember.

JAMES. You've got a willow-pattern tea set, I know that.

JULIE. First thing I bought with my Saturday money… first grown-up thing I ever owned. An old ladies' tea set.

ANDY. And I had the mugs, my mum used to give me cocoa in a willow-pattern mug, and tell me the story…

JULIE. When I was fifteen I thought it was the most beautiful thing I'd ever seen.

It's a classic.

It's beautiful.

And it *still* sells…

I just want to hold onto one thing, James… that's…

Sees he's not getting it.

It's because of the story…

JAMES. What story?

JULIE. See, I *told* you the story...

ANDY. Oh, tell him the story! The story's brilliant!

JULIE. Everything on the plate is a story... I told you this and you don't even remember! Why should I tell you this again!

ANDY. Aw, because it's brilliant! Every time I was sick, Mum told me this story.

   JULIE *starts to tell the story. Upset, not looking at* JAMES.

JULIE. A rich Chinese merchant fiddled his taxes...

ANDY. He'd fiddled his taxes and he'd fiddled his customs duty.

JULIE. So he takes himself off into hiding in his big country house with his daughter and his secretary.

   And the secretary and the daughter fall in love.

   Her father finds out. He's not happy. He throws the young secretary out of the house...

   But the young man's in love. He keeps sneaking back to see the daughter. They build a big fence to keep him out...

ANDY. You can see it at the bottom of the plate.

JULIE. Then the daughter is to be married off to another rich man, a duke... The duke brings her a big box of jewels the night before her wedding, all she can do is sit and cry. But her lover sneaks in with the wedding party.

   They take the jewels... they run away, over the bridge between the island and the shore... they get away.

ANDY. There she is with her spinning. There's the clever secretary with the box of jewels. There's her dad chasing them with a whip. You can see it all there on the plate in blue and white.

JULIE. They're living happily ever after on an island of their own.

ANDY. Why could it no stop there?

JULIE. But the duke the girl was supposed to marry is raging angry. He doesn't stop looking for them. He finds them, he kills the boy. The girl locks herself in the house and sets it on fire, the house, the jewels, the girl, they all go up together…

JAMES. Is there a point to this story?

JULIE. It's…

ANDY. It's romantic… it's about true love…

JULIE. It's just…

She's too upset.

ANDY. *That's* the kind of girl you want! One that'll risk everything to be with you!

JULIE. They risked everything…

JAMES. They robbed a bloody duke…

JULIE. Yes!

JAMES. Could've just legged it. No need for the larceny, was there?

JULIE. Yes! Because they wanted the same things!

JAMES. What? True love and a drawer stuffed with diamonds?

JULIE. Yes.

Yes. Why not? Why not, James?

(*Quiet.*) Diamonds are beautiful…

The gods took pity on them. They forgave them. They took those two lovers and turned them into bluebirds. Two kissing bluebirds…

JULIE *can't go on.*

ANDY. 'Of course that's not really a Chinese story,' says Maddy. 'It's just a bit of marketing made up by the English potteries when they started copying Chinese designs.'

JAMES. Why did you tell me this story?

JULIE. Do you *remember* me telling you this story?

JAMES. No.

Why did you tell me this story?

JULIE. You broke my teacup.

JAMES. I did?

JULIE. I was away. That conference weekend. I came back and you'd made every plate in the place dirty. And even then you didn't do the washing-up, you didn't rinse a mug, you just pulled out my willow-pattern china, pulled the tissue paper off it and threw your tea and whisky into that. And then you dropped it in the sink with the pans on top of it.

JAMES. I said sorry, though…

JULIE. No. You didn't. I tried to tell you this story. What it meant to me. Why I was upset… and you didn't hear me. I could see you trying to listen with one eye on the telly and half your mind down the morgue… and you didn't get it. You just didn't hear me…

And the next night, some of the boys were going for a drink so I did. And when I went to leave they said, 'Stay, Julie, come on, you're always dashing off.' And I thought I am, I'm always dashing off home for a life I hope will be waiting by the fire for me, a man waiting with a smile and a cuddle and a day that's not been as stressed out as mine. But it's never there. Either there's no one there at all or there's just James with his bad bad day needing to be put to bed… His bad day, worse than mine could ever be, always…

Love and money, James.

I deserve both and you were never going to give me either.

So I stayed in the pub that night.

And I met Andy.

And I told him about my tea set. I told him the story… And he loved it already.

ANDY. My mum…

(*Upset.*) Mum used to give me cocoa in my willow-pattern mug, when I was sick…

JAMES. Well, you're obviously soulmates.

JULIE. No. I don't think he wants me after all.

ANDY. I do! Oh Christ, I do, Julie! I can see it! I can see it now! It's you! It's just you! I'll live for you! I'm so sick! Save me, Julie!

JAMES. I don't think you can come back, Julie.

JULIE. I don't want to come back.

What are you going to do?

JAMES. About what?

JULIE. You opened the boxes. You found the rugs.

JAMES. I did.

ANDY. He *did*? Oh Christ, we're dead.

JULIE. Was that all that was in there, James? Just rugs?

JAMES. I only took one out… Why are you asking that?

ANDY. Why are you asking that?

JULIE *doesn't answer.*

JAMES. Do you know who you left me for, Julie? Andy Telfer's mum was fencing stolen goods when wee Andy was still hanging off her tit.

ANDY. She had nothing and she still kept us like princes! Don't you fucking judge her, you bastard!

JULIE. He told me they were just fiddling a bit of duty.

JAMES. And what are they doing?

ANDY. Oh Christ. Oh Christ, Julie darling, it'll be the last bit of darkness before we can buy sunlight for ever.

It's the boy's fault! I thought he knew what he was doing. I didn't know they were playing him. I didn't know what they were up to till they caught me the next day with my hangover and put the real deal on the table. When those guys put a deal on the table you *can't* say no…

Swaying.

Oh… I'm not feeling… oh, this is no good…

JULIE. I need to get out of here.

JAMES. You need a lift?

JULIE. I'll get a taxi.

ANDY. Taxi? What happened to the van? Julie? *Where's the stock? Where are my boxes?!*

JAMES. Are you okay? Julie? What's happened?

ANDY. Julie, what happened?

JULIE. I'm in a mess. Need to get myself out of it.

JAMES. So come back to the station with me.

ANDY. No!

JULIE. No. I need to fix this myself.

JAMES. Julie.

Julie, God help me… I still don't want to see you come to harm. Tell me what's going on.

JULIE. I can't.

But I am sorry, James.

JAMES. Yeah. I know.

JAMES *is writing something out. He hands her a bit of paper.*

Here.

JULIE. What's that?

JAMES. That's the number of the police department you should call, when you're ready to confess all. When you've decided to tell everything. Ring them.

JULIE. Or you will?

JAMES. Kind of have to.

JULIE. Yeah. Yeah, of course.

ANDY. Julie?… I'm not feeling right… I'm… oh… no… I don't want to…

ANDY is back in the bed, unconscious.

JULIE. How long have I got?

JAMES. Twenty-four hours, tops.

He exits.

JULIE takes ANDY's hand and starts to cry.

Fade lights into: Cherry trees beaten down by heavy rain.

By the office door in the dark.

LIN HAN is sitting on the doorstep. It is raining. She is wet. She is crying quietly.

She has opened the box of rugs. She has wrapped herself in a panda rug for warmth.

She has found little boxes of perfume in the crate. They are scattered around her.

JIE HUI limps out of the dark and the rain. He is sodden, bleeding. He has been beaten up. He stops when he sees LIN HAN.

JIE HUI. Hullo.

LIN HAN just watches him.

Why are you crying?

LIN HAN. It's the rain, on my face.

> You can see the cherry trees in The Meadows. The rain is making the petals fall. There's nothing beautiful here any more.

> JIE HUI *moves closer to her.*

> Why are you bleeding?

JIE HUI. It's nothing.

LIN HAN. It's something. Your face is broken.

JIE HUI. Lin Han…

LIN HAN. Yes?

JIE HUI. Lin Han… I am not a bad person… it's just I made bad friends.

LIN HAN. So…

> You don't think you're lying when you say that. I can see that.

JIE HUI. It's true.

LIN HAN. Who thinks they are a bad person? Even people who laugh like villains think they are misunderstood.

> They think they have no choice.

> They think they have to torture and break hearts.

JIE HUI. I haven't hurt anyone.

LIN HAN. Look at me. I'm hurt.

JIE HUI. Why are you crying?

LIN HAN. You lied to me.

JIE HUI. Yes.

LIN HAN. I don't even know what you lied to me about.

JIE HUI. I'm sorry.

LIN HAN. How badly are you injured because if you are bleeding to death this is not the time for this conversation.

JIE HUI. I'm fine I just…

LIN HAN. Do you have a bandage… a cloth to wipe the blood…?

JIE HUI. Yes I…

He fishes out a handkerchief. Tries to wipe blood.

LIN HAN. Because it's distracting watching you bleed.

JIE HUI. I just need to… sit down…

She makes space for him in the doorway.

He sits beside her. She hands him another handkerchief.

Thank you.

After a moment she takes it from him and mops at his face.

LIN HAN. Who did this to you?

JIE HUI. They're from Montrose.

LIN HAN. That means nothing to me.

JIE HUI. They're the brothers of a friend of mine.

LIN HAN. What friend?

JIE HUI. Susie.

LIN HAN. I don't understand.

JIE HUI. I was stupid. They made a fool of me. The goods were… we paid you a fair price.

LIN HAN. I don't understand.

JIE HUI. We showed you our costs. They were all accurate. The shipping, the marketing… the duty we had to pay…

LIN HAN. I don't understand.

JIE HUI. The duty was not paid. I thought that was what they were doing.

LIN HAN. No… I don't understand.

JIE HUI. I thought we were just fiddling a little bit of tax. No harm done… but… You were a cover load.

LIN HAN. A cover load.

JIE HUI. Susie introduced me to her brothers. They had the shipping contacts… the trucking contacts… they were cheap… I just thought I was getting you a good price… I promise you I didn't know.

(*Explains*.) They put other things in the containers.

LIN HAN. I know.

JIE HUI. You know?

LIN HAN. I found a box. These are under the rugs.

She shows him the little boxes of perfume.

(*Reading the English*.) Calvin Klein 'Beauty', Chloé 'Love'…

JIE HUI. Lin Han…

LIN HAN. Gucci 'Guilt'…

JIE HUI. They're counterfeit. It's big money.

LIN HAN. I know. I know what they are.

She lifts a tag from one of the perfume boxes and holds it out to him.

(*Reading, quiet and sad*.) 'Give the gift of love.'

JIE HUI takes the tag from her.

JIE HUI. Lin Han, I've lost your stock.

Andy was shot. Perhaps they shot him. I think they shot him.

But they wanted to know where he was…

LIN HAN. They hit you to find out where he was?

JIE HUI. Yes.

LIN HAN. Did you tell them?

JIE HUI. I told them I didn't want to be part of their plan to smuggle things inside your crates of rugs! So they hit me. A lot.

Andy's safe in hospital anyway.

I've lost your stock, I've lost your money…

LIN HAN. I still don't understand.

JIE HUI. Andy was going to pay you! I can't pay you…!

LIN HAN (*interrupts*). No. I don't understand about Susie.

JIE HUI *drops his head*. LIN HAN *waits*.

JIE HUI. Susie was my girlfriend.

We just split up.

LIN HAN. So, she was your girlfriend when you were writing to me?

JIE HUI. Yes.

LIN HAN. How could you do that?

JIE HUI. I was just being friendly.

You sounded friendly.

You made me feel warm.

Susie's very cold.

LIN HAN. But you love her.

JIE HUI. I can't help it.

She's almost perfect.

LIN HAN. Tell me about her being perfect.

JIE HUI. No.

LIN HAN. Tell me about her being perfect.

JIE HUI. She's an air hostess. That's how I met her.

She has wonderful hair, white, she dyes it, I think, but it would be pale anyway.

She's got skin like ice cream.

She smells amazing. Never the same twice. Her room's full of shining bottles... I thought it was duty free.

Her room is neat and white and shining, like her.

I never know what she's thinking.

I'll talk and talk and tell her every plan in my head and she just watches.

Sometimes she smiles, just a small neat smile that never shows her teeth.

But I never know what's in her head. I never see myself in her eyes, in her thoughts. I can't stop loving her until she sees me.

I want her so much. It makes no sense that she doesn't want me back.

I want to see her pale eyes looking at me. I want her to see me at last.

That's all.

LIN HAN. Yes.

That's the way I love people too.

You don't know her at all.

She was probably thinking about her breakfast or what to watch on television.

She was probably thinking how to fool you.

She's a criminal.

She was using you.

JIE HUI. Yes.

LIN HAN. That's not perfect. That's not even very good.

JIE HUI. No.

LIN HAN. You don't know her but you want her.

JIE HUI. I wish I didn't.

I didn't tell you about my girlfriend and I've lost your money
and your rugs and I've been making deals with serious
criminals who torture people… but I haven't killed anyone.

LIN HAN (*bitter*). Yes, that's the good news.

JIE HUI. I'll pay you back. I won't rob your father. I promise
you. If I have to clean floors my whole life I'll pay him back.
I'll find your rugs. I'll kick that door in and take out every
piece of paper. I'll find your money. I'll break the lock…
I'll…

LIN HAN (*interrupts*). The door is open.

JIE HUI. The door's open!?

LIN HAN. Yes, but there's no one there.

JIE HUI *gets up and pulls the door open.* JULIE *is right on
the other side with her arms full of boxes and papers. She
shrieks and drops some of them.* LIN HAN *and* JIE HUI
shriek and leap back. They all stare at each other.

JULIE. Tell me I didny just drop the laptop.

*Looks, she hasn't. Sighs with relief. Starts reorganising
boxes.*

Thought you were the customs guys, someone was snooping
around a while back, I've been hiding in there for hours.

LIN HAN. Who is she?

JULIE (*glaring at* JIE HUI). You! *You!* You dropped us right in
it, you bastard!

JIE HUI. I didn't know!

JULIE. Well, you should have known! How stupid are you?!

JIE HUI. Andy should have known! I was in love!

JULIE. How stupid are you?

LIN HAN. Stop shouting at us!

JULIE. Andy nearly got killed!

JIE HUI. He's alive? How is he?

JULIE. He's alive. No thanks to you.

He's alive but his company isn't.

JIE HUI. It's not?

JULIE. I just killed it. Emptied the bank accounts transferred the assets. So when Her Majesty's Revenue and Customs get here they can help themselves to nothing at all.

JIE HUI. You killed his company?

But you work for Andy?

JULIE. *With!*

I never worked 'for'. Equal partners, that was the deal. I had his PIN numbers, I wrote his signature more often than he did. I had his trust. Now I've got his money and my own company.

LIN HAN. Who is she?

JULIE *ignores this, just focused on* JIE HUI.

JULIE. What? Why are you looking at me like that? You think I'm shafting my Andy? Stabbing him in the back? What are you doing here anyway?

LIN HAN. What is she doing here?

JIE HUI. Looking for our rugs!

JULIE. Your bloody girlfriend's got our rugs! Or her brothers have.

JIE HUI. You had our rugs!

JULIE. They took them off me! In the hospital car park! They took the van. Do you know the day I've had?

LIN HAN. She knows where the rugs are?

JULIE. Well, do you?

You know he was on at me and on at me to leave James. Come to him. Love him. Make money with him. Be with him… and then I turn up on his doorstep this morning…

He's trying to look delighted but he just looks like… like someone promised him a bunch of roses, and now they've turned up with a big prickly cactus and he's worried he's going to have to pay for it.

And then all he wants to know is why I've left the bloody boxes behind.

So I get them but I've nowhere to put them. I'm driving round and round… and then I get the call telling me he's half-dead in the hospital.

So I drive the wrong way round a roundabout. I canny see which way is up I'm that distraught and I get a ticket… and by the time I'm done with that and get up to the hospital… Those two *animals*, your girlfriend's half-human sibling scum are waiting… they're *waiting* for me… they grabbed me! In broad daylight!!

Shows him.

Bruises!!

And they were smuggling stuff in my lovely rugs! And they probably already shot my Andy!

JIE HUI. Yes. Yes, I know.

JULIE. And it's your fault we even know them!

*JULIE starts hitting him with whatever she has to hand.
LIN HAN stops her.*

LIN HAN (*in English*). No! Stop!

(*To* JIE HUI, *in Mandarin*.) Who is she?

JULIE. You stay out of this. Who are you anyway?

JIE HUI. The rugs are hers. Her family makes them.

JULIE. Oh!

She stops. Her whole mood changes. She turns all her attention on LIN HAN.

Oh, I'm so glad to meet you. I'm sorry. I'm so glad to see you...

This is the nastiest, *ugliest* day I've ever known and it shouldn't have been. It should never have been like this because your rugs...

She takes LIN HAN*'s hands.*

Your rugs are the most beautiful things... the most *beautiful* things...

Turns to JIE HUI.

Can you see they're beautiful?

JIE HUI. They're nice rugs.

JULIE. Could that cold-faced, criminal girlfriend of yours?

JIE HUI. She's not my girlfriend!

JULIE. No. And she wouldn't know beautiful if she didn't see it in the mirror. Her own snow face.

Andy didn't either.

I found the rugs. *I* picked them out of his stock samples. *I* knew they were beautiful. I knew I could sell them and I will sell them.

Here.

She hands paper to LIN HAN.

I'm so glad you're here.

(*To* JIE HUI.) Tell her I'm glad she's here.

LIN HAN (*in English*). I understand.

JULIE. Your rugs are *beautiful*.

LIN HAN. Thank you.

JULIE. I am going to sell them because they're beautiful. I
would *never* use your boxes to smuggle rubbish. I want your
beautiful rugs. Real marketable beauty.

Sorting the papers she's giving LIN HAN.

This is a banker's draft.

This is my company name… sorry there's a few typos in
that… and this is my card… watch it doesny smudge, ink's
still a bit damp.

Do we have a deal?

LIN HAN *hesitates, bemused.*

JIE HUI. She can't sell your rugs. She doesn't have your rugs.

JULIE. Shut it, you.

JIE HUI (*in Mandarin*). She has nothing.

(*In English.*) She's making a deal with nothing!

LIN HAN (*in Mandarin*). Be quiet!

She's looking intently at JULIE.

(*Quiet.*) Say again, please.

JULIE *is looking straight into* LIN HAN*'s eyes. Slow and
sincere –*

JULIE. I love your rugs.

I will find your rugs.

I will sell your rugs.

And I will never, ever, cheat you.

Do we have a deal?

LIN HAN (*hesitant*). Yes… I think… Yes.

JULIE. Brilliant!

She shakes LIN HAN*'s hand, then impulsively kisses her.*

(*To* JIE HUI.) Right, you, help me carry the rest of this stuff to my car.

JIE HUI. You don't have the rugs. You don't know where they are.

JULIE. No, but your girlfriend does. She doesn't want them, does she?

Her brothers will have already taken out what they want.

Give me her address.

JIE HUI. They'll kill you!

JULIE. Do I look like I care now?!

Give me her address!

JIE HUI. What do you think they'll do if you go there alone! You're crazy!

JULIE. Give me her address or I'll show you exactly how crazy I am!

JIE HUI *starts writing on the tag* LIN HAN *gave him.*

(*Really upset.*) The folk at the hospital think Andy might die.

He might die and he lied to me.

When I think of him dead there's this big hole, right in the heart of me, where all my hope, all my idea of the future, of loving, being loved, is just dust and rubble.

When I think how he lied to me I can actually feel my heart shrivelling up and turning bitter as mouldy lemons.

But you know what? If that's what I've got to go through, I'm fucked if I'm going through it poor. I'd *rather* they killed me.

And you know what?

She snatches the tag off JIE HUI *and throws it down.*

I don't have to do this alone. You can bloody *show* me where she is. You *owe* me.

JIE HUI (*quiet*). Yes.

JULIE. Yes. So pick up that box.

JULIE *exits.*

A world of wet cherry tree blossom.

JIE HUI *picks up the box and hesitates.*

JIE HUI (*to* LIN HAN). At least she paid you.

LIN HAN. Yes.

JIE HUI. You can go home now.

LIN HAN. Yes.

LIN HAN *is picking at the papers* JULIE *has abandoned.*

JIE HUI. I have to see her again. I have to face her.

LIN HAN. Of course. But she doesn't love you.

JIE HUI. No.

LIN HAN. I'm not sorry I am leaving but I'm sorry I'm leaving as a fool.

JIE HUI. You're not a fool.

LIN HAN. If you love someone but they do not love you back you are a fool.

JIE HUI. I'm sorry… you are… I do think you are…

LIN HAN (*stopping him*). *Don't!*

If you were very good-looking at least, that would be something. But I liked you because you were just good-looking enough to match me.

If you were as beautiful as a movie star, or if you had done something extraordinary, or if you were a hero… then I would not be an idiot to love you when you do not love me back.

JIE HUI. You said…

> You said you didn't love me. You said you wanted me to love you first.

LIN HAN. You understand nothing. No wonder your girlfriend made a fool of you.

JIE HUI. She's not my…

LIN HAN. Are you going to do something extraordinary!?

JIE HUI. You mean… *now*?

LIN HAN. Of course now! What other time do we have!?

> *JIE HUI stares at her, completely at a loss.*

> *A car horn sounds offstage.*

> No. I didn't think so.

> *JIE HUI exits.*

> *LIN HAN picks up the tag and reads it again.*

> 'The gift of true love.'

> *She puts it down on the scattered boxes of counterfeit perfume. She exits.*

> *Fade lights into: The green bamboo forests, brilliant, fresh-green dappled shade. We hear the panda call, closer than ever and then, somewhere above in the leaves, a chirruping returned call.*

> *A hotel room in the Panda Province, China.*

> *MADELEINE is standing, looking out the small window. There's a knock at the door. She opens it. JAMES is there.*

MADELEINE. Oh!

> *They stare at each other for a moment.*

JAMES. Can I come in?

> *MADELEINE stands back to let him come in.*

He looks round the room.

Small.

MADELEINE. Not for the price.

JAMES sits down on the bed.

JAMES. Thought it would be easier to find you. It took me days.

MADELEINE. Have you come to take me back?

JAMES. Can I put my head down for a bit? I'm absolutely whacked.

MADELEINE. Yes… of course.

JAMES lies back. MADELEINE looks at him then goes back to looking out the window.

LIN HAN and JIE HUI occupy the same space but they are back in the hotel in Edinburgh.

LIN HAN is packing, sniffing mournfully. JIE HUI appears at the window. He's climbed up the wall outside.

LIN HAN sees him. She screams.

He's gesturing at her frantically.

Finally she gets it, she opens the window to let him in.

She helps pull him into the room. He lies on the floor, breathless.

LIN HAN. What are you doing here? Are you crazy!?

JIE HUI (*breathless*). Something… extraordinary…

LIN HAN. What?

JIE HUI. Lin Han, you are a very beautiful, very special girl… I don't want you to feel stupid… I wanted to show you… I wanted to do this extraordinary thing.

LIN HAN. Climbing two floors up the outside of the Haymarket Travelodge?

JIE HUI. I counted… three…

LIN HAN. That is not extraordinary! That is stupid! That is insane!

But thank you, yes, thank you! This is a big help in falling out of love with you because I don't want to love a crazy stupid person!

Plus it was not that high. If you fell you might not even die.

JIE HUI. I choose to love you.

Everything you say is what you are thinking. It's what you really mean, I don't have to guess. It's perfect. You're perfect.

I'm tired of being cold. I'm tired of holding ice and being wet and cold. I thought I was in love and I was just betrayed. I was just an idiot.

I told her. I told her I'd never be a fool like that again.

I was ready to face her brothers…

LIN HAN. You fought the men who hurt you?

JIE HUI. I would have done. The police came so we had to get away but… I'll be a hero for you! I'll be extraordinary. I promise. I'll follow you anywhere.

I love you.

LIN HAN. So.

Alright.

You are very very very late. Now I have to think what I really want.

Lie down then. Lie down here. You've nearly killed yourself.

JIE HUI *lies down on the bed.*

JAMES *wakes up.*

MADELEINE. Is he dead?

JAMES. Not when I left.

MADELEINE. He should have realised I was dangerous. I chose not to be dangerous because I loved him.

That's not the same thing as being bland.

At all.

The truth is, revenge does make you feel better. It makes me feel better. It really really does.

I'd rather be wicked than forgiving.

JAMES. It was a heart attack.

MADELEINE. Sorry?

JAMES. He's got a bruised arse but that's not what laid him out. His heart couldn't take the shock.

You weren't to know.

Still potentially manslaughter if he pegs out, of course.

MADELEINE. Are you arresting me?

JAMES. Takes fucking weeks to sort out extradition.

MADELEINE. Does it?

JAMES. I listened to the tape.

MADELEINE. Yes.

JAMES. My name's James.

MADELEINE. James.

JAMES. I'm on holiday as it happens. Always fancied seeing the Great Wall of China up close.

MADELEINE. It's seven hundred miles away.

JAMES. Right...

What is there to see round here then?

MADELEINE. This town.

JAMES. Is it all like this?

MADELEINE. Pretty much.

JAMES. It's very… grey.

MADELEINE. I like it. Every so often you see something red, and you notice it's the most beautiful red you've ever seen.

The mountains are beautiful.

And the bamboo forests.

You won't see any pandas.

You can see me.

JAMES. Yes.

Julie… my…

Pause. He can't go on.

MADELEINE. Who's Julie?

JAMES. She's my wife. She left me.

She's…

She's…

MADELEINE. She's…?

JAMES. She's importing rugs. From China.

MADELEINE. Oh?

(Realisation.) Oh!

JAMES. So…

MADELEINE. So… that's why you're here?

JAMES. I don't know.

MADELEINE. You're here for *your* revenge.

JAMES. I don't know.

MADELEINE. Aw, fuck…

JAMES. What?

MADELEINE. I thought… I really thought… there was a… something… between us.

JAMES. Yes.

MADELEINE. But you're after a revenge shag.

JAMES. Well… maybe…

MADELEINE. Aren't you?

JAMES. How can I tell?

MADELEINE. Wait… wait… let me work this out.

ANDY and JULIE occupy the same space but they're in the hospital room.

ANDY comes round.

ANDY. Hullo.

JULIE. Hullo.

ANDY. It's you!

JULIE. Yes.

ANDY. You're here!

JULIE. Yes, your mother was here too but she had to sort some business.

ANDY. But you're here!

Julie, was I dead?

JULIE. Nearly.

ANDY. I know. I know I was. I was outside myself. I could see everything. I understood everything. And I understood that it's you, Julie, here and now, it's you. I love you.

JULIE. Andy, I've taken all your money.

Pause.

ANDY. Where from?

JULIE. I've emptied your accounts into mine.

Beat.

ANDY. The ones you knew about.

JULIE. Sorry?

ANDY. Did you find any accounts you didn't know about before?

JULIE. No.

ANDY. Beijing? Shanghai?

JULIE. No.

ANDY. No, you've got some of my money. From the accounts you know about. The daily-use ones.

JULIE. You've got others?

ANDY. What do you take me for?

JULIE. So I've got half your money?

ANDY. Maybe. You've got what the tax man knew about. About a third.

Pause.

JULIE. Right… okay… right…

Let me think about this…

In her space, MADELEINE *is still looking out the window.*

JAMES. Madeleine?

MADELEINE. Wait… I'm thinking… wait…

LIN HAN *is close to* JIE HUI.

LIN HAN. When I wake up in the morning. I look out my window and this is what I see…

I see the road that the trucks roar down on the way to the city, a mist of blue diesel, pink and blue bags tied to the sides of the trucks.

I see the peach trees across the road, leaning over the highway. They'll still be bare but the tips of their wooden fingers will be fat with the promise of leaves.

I see three dusty, dark horses that my neighbour uses to take tourists up the river. They all have pale muzzles from mumbling the dust as they wait. One is a little bigger and his saddle is red. He is the best one.

I see the clinic. The door is still closed. Its yellow sign is bright above the dark bolted door and the dark shuttered window. If I ever see the door open I'm late or sick. I'm never sick and I've never been in the clinic but I've chatted to the nurse in the door on my way home from work.

She smells of disinfectant and the skin on her hands is split with washing too much in cold water.

Behind the clinic is the hill. It's a humble little hill like a big stray dog curled up, hunched against the cold.

It's brown and mangy now but in a few weeks it will flush green and be so much taller with proud leaves.

There are white moths in the leaves and some of them make it across the road, blown by the wake of the trucks and get caught in the mesh at my window.

I can hear my mother banging the stove and my father spitting in the sink.

I love this place.

You will think it's very small.

I want to go home so much.

But I still don't want to leave you. It's making me angry.

JIE HUI. I choose to love you. I'll follow you anywhere.

LIN HAN. You've left it very late. I think my flight will be full.

JIE HUI. That's alright.

LIN HAN. I won't change my seat, I'm sitting exactly where I wanted to sit. I have to be in the tail because that's the best place. You're more likely to survive a crash in the tail and I have to sit on the aisle so I can turn my ankles like this to keep my circulation even. If you can't get a seat next to me I won't change my seat.

JIE HUI. Alright.

LIN HAN. You can come from where you're sitting and talk to me. Once the seat-belt sign is off.

JIE HUI. Alright.

LIN HAN. You can meet my mother and father.

JIE HUI. Good.

LIN HAN. That's all I can promise you.

JIE HUI. That's good.

LIN HAN. Alright.

Beat. Then abruptly she kisses him passionately.

Oh, you bastard. Now I really love you. You're hurting me so much already.

Never mind.

JIE HUI. I won't ever hurt you.

LIN HAN. You will. You'll break me into bits. I've seen the films.

It doesn't matter.

It will make me smile when I'm very old. Let's look forward to that.

JIE HUI. You're crazy.

LIN HAN. Love's crazy. I just accept it.

He kisses her again.

JAMES *has come close to* MADELEINE.

JAMES. Madeleine… when we were in that interview room… I wasn't expecting to feel anything. I wasn't looking to feel anything but when you touched me…

He can't go on, they're close together, bristling sexual tension.

And you didn't know…

MADELEINE. Know what?

(*Realises.*) Oh, that my ex had left me for your ex?

JAMES. Yeah.

MADELEINE. No… no… I mean, I knew I was in a heightened emotional state, obviously.

JAMES. Obviously.

MADELEINE. But… I… just really fancied you, not the moment I saw you…

JAMES. No.

MADELEINE. About when… when you got me a drink of water.

JAMES. Yes. When I got you the water. I saw you.

MADELEINE. Yes. And I really thought… hoped… that you fancied me back.

JAMES. I really fancy you.

Really.

MADELEINE. Oh, that's brilliant.

But you suspect your motives.

JAMES. I do.

MADELEINE. But you were driven to fly thousands of miles to check them out.

JAMES. I was.

Pause.

MADELEINE. Aw, fuck, that's good enough to get going, isn't it?

JAMES. Yeah.

They grab for each other – raw passion.

JULIE. Customs were watching you, Andy.

ANDY. Shit! I knew that inspection wasn't a coincidence. Did they give you a hard time?

JULIE. They tried. But I persuaded them to save the real hard time for you.

ANDY. I can dodge them. Did they get the rugs?

JULIE. No. I'd already got the rugs.

ANDY. How'd you get the rugs?

JULIE. I was psychopathic.

ANDY. Oh… right.

I always knew you'd save my business.

JULIE. It's my business.

ANDY. Aye, but… you stole it from me.

JULIE. No. You owe me.

ANDY. For what!?

JULIE. Anguish, torment, deception, stress…

ANDY. It's all part of a relationship, Julie! Alright, you can have the business! You can have whatever you want.

JULIE. You think we're making a deal here?

ANDY. Aren't we?

Beat.

JULIE. No more lies.

ANDY. Okay.

JULIE. Nothing dodgy. Ever again.

ANDY. No. I promise.

JULIE. And when you break that promise it's on your books. It doesn't come near me.

ANDY. Never.

JULIE. And I furnish the house on your shilling.

ANDY. All the beautiful things you want.

JULIE. Okay.

(*Complete change of ton*e.) Oh, Andy darling, I thought you were dead!

She embraces him. JAMES *and* MADELEINE *slow down.*

MADELEINE. Are you staying?

JAMES. Do you care?

MADELEINE. Not right now.

JAMES. I'm staying. I want to stay. I want to see everything.

ANDY. Mind my stitches! Oh, Julie darling…

JULIE. Don't you ever get yourself killed again!

JIE HUI. Will I see pandas?

LIN HAN. Only the ones in the sanctuary. They aren't real pandas.

They've bred them like dogs and they sit in big puzzled herds in little fields. Real pandas live alone. They never come near another panda unless they want to mate.

JAMES. Will I see pandas shagging?

MADELEINE. No one ever does.

LIN HAN. They hardly ever mate. They wait for the right panda.

JULIE. Andy, if we don't have true love and pots of money after all this, *I'll* kill you!

ANDY. You're my luck. You're the coin toss I can't lose. You're the one. God, you're *perfect*!

They embrace again.

JIE HUI. So, what's the right panda?

LIN HAN. The panda that loves the way they do.

MADELEINE. They wait up trees, watching other pandas pass below. They wait a long time for the panda worth climbing out of the tree for. No one ever sees them touch each other.

JULIE. I didn't know I had this in me, I'm not changing back now!

ANDY. I don't want you to change. Ever.

JAMES. I wanted to see pandas.

MADELEINE. I can show you a slide of the little flea that lives in the warm follicle of panda fur. I can show you that.

JULIE. Alright. So what happens now?

ANDY. Now we can sell some rugs.

MADELEINE. James, promise me, as long as we can, five mad minutes or... however long we can... let's be good to each other.

JAMES. I promise.

JIE HUI. Listen, I know I've switched around like a coin flicked over on the table. I know you want a romantic moment and you're so sad that I can't bring you a fresh one. You deserve that, but...

There are so many romantic moments... it's what happens once they've died away. How we behave after the death of passion, that's what makes it a happy ending or a waste of love.

LIN HAN. Endings are for weaklings.

The trees surge in the wind, the leaves move, the lush green bamboo forest covers everything.

And then, climbing down through the leaves, looking down, the briefest clear glimpse...

The panda face looking out through the bamboo leaves...

End of play.

Debbie Tucker Green
BORN BAD
DIRTY BUTTERFLY
RANDOM
STONING MARY
TRADE & GENERATIONS

Liz Lochhead
BLOOD AND ICE
DRACULA *after* Stoker
EDUCATING AGNES ('The School for Wives') *after* Molière
GOOD THINGS
MARY QUEEN OF SCOTS GOT HER HEAD CHOPPED OFF
MEDEA *after* Euripides
MISERYGUTS ('The Miser') & TARTUFFE *after* Molière
PERFECT DAYS
THEBANS *after* Euripides & Sophocles

Linda McLean
ANY GIVEN DAY
ONE GOOD BEATING
RIDDANCE
SHIMMER
STRANGERS, BABIES

Rona Munro
THE HOUSE OF BERNARDA ALBA *after* Lorca
THE INDIAN BOY
IRON
THE LAST WITCH
LITTLE EAGLES
LONG TIME DEAD
THE MAIDEN STONE
MARY BARTON *after* Gaskell
STRAWBERRIES IN JANUARY *from* de la Chenelière
YOUR TURN TO CLEAN THE STAIR & FUGUE

Joanna Murray-Smith
BOMBSHELLS
THE FEMALE OF THE SPECIES
HONOUR

Amanda Whittington
BE MY BABY
LADIES' DAY
LADIES DOWN UNDER
SATIN 'N' STEEL

A Nick Hern Book

Pandas first published in Great Britain in 2011 as a paperback original by Nick Hern Books Limited, 14 Larden Road, London W3 7ST, in association with the Traverse Theatre, Edinburgh

Cover photograph by Euan Myles
Cover design by Ned Hoste, 2H

Typeset by Nick Hern Books, London
Printed in Great Britain by CLE Print Ltd, St Ives, Cambs, PE27 3LE

ISBN 978 1 84842 196 7

A CIP catalogue record for this book is available from the British Library